Richard Crisp is Professor of Psychology at the Aston Business School and a prolific scientist and author. Twenty years ago, at Oxford University, he was introduced to the wonderful world of psychological science. The experience inspired a quest to understand how society shapes our behaviour, beliefs, attitudes and values. Now with a distinguished academic record and many of the discipline's highest accolades and awards, he is regarded as one of the world's leading experts on the psychology of social and cultural diversity.

He was the 2012 winner of the Society for the Psychological Study of Social Issues Gordon Allport Intergroup Relations Prize (for the best paper of the year on intergroup relations), 2013 winner of the British Psychological Society Social Psychology Section Mid-Career Prize (for outstanding research in social psychology) and 2014 winner of the British Psychological Society Presidents' Award for Distinguished Contributions to Psychological Knowledge. He is also a past winner of the British Psychological Society Spearman Medal and has been recognised with election to Fellow of the Academy of Social Sciences, Fellow of the Association for Psychological Science and Fellow of the British Psychological Society. He is the author of the introductory textbook *Essential Social Psychology* and Editor-in-Chief of the *Journal of Applied Social Psychology*.

THE SOCIAL BRAIN

Richard Crisp

ROBINSON

ROBINSON

First published in Great Britain in 2015 by Robinson

A CIP catalogue record for this book
is available from the British Library.

ISBN 978-1-47212-023-6 (paperback)
ISBN: 978-1-47212-024-3 (ebook)

Typeset in Times by Photoprint, Torquay
Printed and bound in Great Britain by Clays Ltd, St Ives plc
Papers used by Robinson are from well-managed forests and other
responsible sources

MIX
Paper from
responsible sources
FSC
www.fsc.org FSC® C104740

Robinson
is an imprint of
Little, Brown Book Group
Carmelite House
50 Victoria Embankment
London EC4Y 0DZ

An Hachette UK Company
www.hachette.co.uk

www.littlebrown.co.uk

To Emilia,
for the delightfully diverse world you've given me

CONTENTS

ACKNOWLEDGEMENTS

Many thanks go to all my students and co-workers over the years. My research adventures have always been collaborative, and the trials and triumphs of scientific discovery have been all the more meaningful because they were shared with significant others.

Thanks to Andrew at Robinson for his careful reading, valuable comments and astute editing.

Thanks to my agent, Diane, for taking me on, driving me forward and keeping me focused.

Lastly, thanks to Kirstie, for her unwavering belief and support (and patience too, particularly when I get a new idea and go on about it all night!).

INTRODUCTION

In 2010, the German chancellor, Angela Merkel, made a widely reported speech to members of her Christian Democratic Union party. In it she announced that attempts to build a multicultural society in Germany had 'utterly failed' and that the 'multikulti' concept, where people live together happily in harmony, simply did not work.[1] This sentiment was echoed in a speech by the British prime minister[2] and has come to characterise much of the political rhetoric surrounding cultural diversity in Western nations.

This rhetoric is not just political polemic – it reflects a public mood. Thirty per cent of Germans reportedly agree with Merkel that their country is 'overrun by foreigners'.[3] In the UK, concerns abound that public services like the NHS, education, social housing and welfare systems have been negatively affected by immigration. A recent survey of thirty thousand Europeans found that 38 per cent of respondents opposed legally established immigrants being granted normal civil rights.[4] In the United States the mood is similar. At the turn of the twentieth century the US accepted large numbers of immigrants with the expectation that they would assimilate and become 'true' Americans. In September 2013, thousands of people protested in one hundred and fifty cities over what they saw as the federal government's weak stance on immigration.[5]

Diversity is a polarising issue. There is a growing gulf between those who extol its virtues and those who believe it is a fundamental cause of instability. Advocates argue that diversity enriches and enhances our culture, providing fertile ground for positive relations, harmony and mutual respect. Opponents point to the realpolitik of intercultural relations: how proximity produces conflict, not peaceful coexistence. For them, diversity is the root cause of disharmony and civic unrest.

This book is about our struggle with diversity – not just in the modern world but throughout our evolution as a species. It's about the psychology that determines why we embrace or eschew cultural differences. It's about the new science that is providing surprising solutions to the 'problem' of diversity. It's about the anthropology that reveals how diversity may have been a critical 'social ecology' from which the adaptability of the human mind was born. It shows how embracing diversity may provide the key to enabling wealth, health, happiness, progress, prosperity and change in the modern world.

A PSYCHOLOGIST'S VIEW

I'm an experimental psychologist, and this is the lens through which I have studied culture, difference and diversity for the last twenty years. Why might psychology prove useful here? Psychology, as a science, has taken great strides in recent years. We can now pinpoint, with incredible accuracy, the origins and the process of human thought. Creative methods and cutting-edge techniques have given us new insights into how we think, feel and understand our place in the world. Neuroscience is taking us beyond the basics – that is, how we see, hear, remember, run, walk and talk. We now understand the complex processes that govern how society, culture and context interact to shape our behaviour, our sense of self, our beliefs, attitudes and ideologies. Each day, new studies shed light on what compels us to support or oppose different political, social and cultural ideals – from the values we hold to the policies we endorse.

I'm going to talk about the psychology of social perception: how who we are and what we think are intimately and intricately linked with the people around us. I'm going to explain the political and public discontent with diversity and suggest why, when the chips are down, people prefer their social worlds to have simplicity and structure. I'll discuss the core psychologies that drive and determine intercultural communication, how humans deal with diversity, and how these psychologies have emerged through the course of human evolution. I'm going to show how intercultural contact has played a pivotal part in the making of the modern mind, how diversity came to define and delimit our attitudes, values and beliefs. I'll argue that previous accounts of human evolution have overlooked a critical element in our ancestors' fight for survival: that our psychologies were forged through cooperation, not just conflict, and that advances in technology, medicine and civic society can all be traced back to the foundations of what might be described as 'coalitional thinking'.

This discussion will reveal a paradox at the heart of diversity politics: how we eschew diversity in all its forms, even though it has played a pivotal part in our past and may well hold the key to our future. It's a paradox predicated upon the evolution of two brain systems, one honed to ensure safety and security, the other to make possible exploration and growth; one to compete, the other to cooperate; one easy and automatic, the other hard to engage. I will argue that for our society to move forward, to evolve and tackle the challenges we face, we must harness the potential of our 'social brain' – that part of us that is cooperative, exploring, engaging. I'll show how the human potential to excel, innovate and overcome is intricately and intimately linked with this social brain system lying latent in the modern psyche.

I'll show that diversity is not simply a moral, ethical or social issue – it's an economic and evolutionary imperative. It's a social ecology that forms the foundation for originality, innovation and growth. Creative thinking is crucial to human development. It helps us to achieve great feats of engineering, forge companies and careers, craft beautiful symphonies and charm potential partners. It is the essence of innovation, the staple of success. We now know a great deal about the psychology that drives creative thinking and, most importantly, the conditions that enable it to be captured, cultivated and grown. I'll show that it is diversity in our social environments that shapes creativity; and, properly harnessed, it can maximise our potential in a whole range of everyday domains.

WHAT'S GONE BEFORE

In his book *Thinking Fast and Slow*[6] Daniel Kahneman describes two distinct systems of thought: one fast and effortless, but flawed; the other slow, effortful but accurate. *The*

Social Brain begins with these systems, and builds around them an expansive theory of how cultural diversity made the modern mind. This theory ties the origins and evolution of human intelligence to the emergence of primitive society in human prehistory. At the same time it incorporates modern experimental psychology in showing how social environments shape our capacity for innovation, progress and growth. It proposes a new way of thinking about social ecologies, and how we can use our social brains to secure successful outcomes in our personal and professional lives.

Throughout the book I'll discuss the scientific evidence that provides support for these ideas as well as the evidence suggesting that to maximise our potential we must embrace diversity in our social worlds. I'll show how, when our social ecologies move beyond our comfort zone and when they challenge norms, expectations, ideologies and beliefs, they can awaken our creative potential; and discuss the ways in which these social ecologies can be structured to activate the social brain, as well as the relationship strategies we can use to enhance creative thinking in different domains.

I will end with speculation on the broader implications of these ideas and suggest how diversity, developed within the fabric of multicultural communities, could forge a prosperous and prolific future. History suggests we are on the right track here, for when societies experience new cultural influences they then undergo periods of intense and significant technological and societal progress. But this change is never easy, and here we find a diversity 'paradox' that lies at the heart of the human condition. This paradox grows from conflict, economic recession and unrest, which compel governments to adopt policies that 'deactivate' the social brain – precisely the part of us that can enable peace, prosperity and progress. Policy designed to switch on the social brain can help not only promote positive relations, but also to harness the creative potential within each and every one of us.

Article 1 of the UNESCO Universal Declaration on Cultural Diversity asserts 'As a source of exchange, innovation and creativity, cultural diversity is as necessary for humankind as biodiversity is for nature'. This book is about the science that shows this assertion to be true. Every step we've taken, whether small or giant, whether in science or in medicine, as a nation or as a species, started as a germ of an idea in the social brain. Our potential to generate new ideas is perhaps our most essential element, but we are only just beginning to understand how it is born through social experience. I hope this book enables that great leap to tie the origins of human society to the making of the modern mind. It is a leap that may ultimately unlock the ingenuity and invention that reside within us all.

CHAPTER 1

DIVERSITY AND ITS DISCONTENTS

A book about diversity should surely start with some statistics. So here we go:

- At the start of the twenty-first century, the world's foreign-born population (those living in a country other than that in which they were born) topped 230 million.[7]

- The number of foreign-born adults (aged 18–34) in the US today has more than doubled since 1980 (1 per cent versus 6 per cent) and one in four (17.9 million) speak a language other than English at home.[8]

- In 1951 the foreign-born population of England and Wales was 1.9 million (4.3 per cent of the total population). In 2011 it had increased to 7.5 million (13 per cent).[9] In London, white British people are already in the minority (45 per cent).[10]

- Over 43,000 hate crimes (e.g. to do with race, sexual orientation, disability) were recorded in England and Wales in 2011–12.[11]

- The Bradford race riots in 2001, some of the worst ever seen in mainland Britain, caused damage estimated at £25 million.[12]

Of course there are, as the saying goes, lies, damned lies and statistics, but trust me (I'm a psychologist). These statistics pretty much sum up the defining characteristics of diversity in modern society. Let's unpack this a little. There are two key things these statistics tell us.

1: Societies are getting more diverse (and it's speeding up).

Whichever way you look at it, as we've developed quicker and more efficient ways to travel the world, it's become easier to settle somewhere other than where we were born. We now live in a world of unprecedented intercultural exchange, where the barriers and boundaries that segregated colour and culture in the twentieth century have all but broken down. In just fifty years Britain has gone from being a largely homogeneous nation in which nationality and race have gone hand in hand, to being decidedly diverse and differentiated. Of course, I focus on Britain because I've had a front-row seat since 1973, but the story is pretty much the same everywhere. In the US, for instance, ethnic-minority groups are growing so quickly that they will be the majority by 2040.[13]

2: Diversity is a big problem.

Hate crimes, race riots, Islamophobia . . . look around – it's increasingly evident that difference and diversity can bring with them conflict, discord and distrust. We're a society struggling with the multicultural ideal. Why does it seem so difficult for humans to just get along? Is there something fundamental to our nature that drives us to reject difference and instead to celebrate the similar, to conform to the norm? Increasingly people seem uneasy – ambivalent at best – with concepts like diversity, multiculturalism and immigration. Of course, most people would not resort to violence, or even voice any unease in public, but it's there – a feeling that, when all's said and done, things would probably be better if everyone was just a little more similar. Can you really get along with someone who comes from an entirely different background, culture and country from yourself?

Multicultural societies appear to be beset by huge inequalities, intolerance and prejudice. A recent influential review of inequality in the United States[14] found that, compared with the white majority, ethnic minority group members are:

- significantly poorer
- under-represented in management and professional occupations
- more likely to be incarcerated
- less likely to own a home
- more likely to drop out of high school
- more likely to suffer from poor health.

While these disparities arise from a complex set of factors, at least some – for instance in areas like income and incarceration – can be explained by racial bias. The UK doesn't fare much better. The 2007 Government Equalities Review concluded that at the current rate of progress it will take until 2080 to elect a culturally representative House of Commons, until 2085 to close the gender pay gap, and until 2105 to close the ethnic employment gap.[15] Unsurprisingly, such disparities lead to high levels of social exclusion. In Germany, Spain and the UK, surveys have shown that most Muslims consider themselves to be primarily Muslims rather than citizens of the country they live in.[16] It seems we are a very long way from the ideal of an integrated, cohesive multicultural society.

These two characteristics of modern society, its increasing diversity and our apparent difficulty in dealing with it, together represent a defining problem of twenty-first-century society, and are the focus of sustained interest by academics, politicians and the media. In 1996 Samuel P. Huntington published a book called *The Clash of Civilizations?*[17] In it he proposed that we are heading irrevocably towards conflict as fundamentally incompatible cultures collide. This analysis fits the state of modern society – tolerance seems a rare entity in this world of discrimination, race riots, stereotyping and prejudice.

So is the story of human history destined to play out this clash of civilisations, an enduring conflict defined by differences in race, religion and ethnicity?

Such a bleak prediction is just one possible future. Here I offer a psychological analysis of the perils and the potential of diversity, one that paints an altogether more complex, and perhaps more positive, picture. It is based upon the psychology that underlies our understanding of diversity: on what drives and determines the opposing views of its value and the impact it has on our everyday lives. It presents a whole new perspective on the diversity debate and the multicultural state, one that not only takes in political, economic and social perspectives, but draws on new and emerging ideas in anthropology, evolution and behavioural neuroscience.

But before all that, a little bit of Freud.

FREUD (IT WASN'T ALL ABOUT SEX)

Talk to most psychological scientists today and they'll tell you that Freud's theories on sexuality and pretty much everything else have been debunked by modern behavioural science (in fact, try it – we get really annoyed when people think psychology is still all psychoanalysis, repressed sexual urges and so on – it's quite something to watch us erupt with indignation). But I'm going to argue he got some things spot on.

In *Civilization and Its Discontents* (1929)[18] Freud sets out the theory that people are fundamentally selfish, driven by their primitive instincts to kill, have sex and eat as much as possible (that sort of thing). What stops us is society; or, more precisely, that part of our brain that constantly reminds us what civilised society expects of us, and what we must not do as a member of that society. Freud argues that there is a fundamental tension between individuals' sex and violence fantasies and the need to repress these desires to function as part of society. Thus, the price of belonging to a civilised society is guilt at these unconscious, unfulfilled egoistic desires, which is then experienced as anxiety or 'discontent'.

This really is a brilliant conceit. It takes an Aristotelian idea of society – that it's a beast of its own, something more than the sum of its peopled parts – and supplants it well and truly in the human mind. This basic idea has proved hugely influential and is one that reverberates through modern social psychology. It also provides a good grounding for what's to follow. We are individuals, but we are social individuals, intimately and intricately connected to each other via morals, values, laws, norms and conventions. Society shapes us, our attitudes, values, goals and beliefs. Our brains are not just brains; they are social brains. This is a key concept that will resonate throughout the book. To understand diversity, we need to look beyond its purely social impact on, say, education, housing and welfare. We need to look to psychological science: the study of how both our real and our remote relationships with others shape our attitudes and behaviour. It is an area of human exploration that is profoundly relevant to everyday life and critical to understanding the past, present and future impact of social and cultural diversity.

EVENTS, NOT PEOPLE, MAKE PEOPLE BAD PEOPLE

The point about a debate is that there are two sides to it. If everyone agreed that diversity was good (or bad) I probably wouldn't be writing this book. An accusation sometimes levelled at those who criticise multiculturalism is that they are racist. So does this mean that the diversity debate is simply driven by people who are racist and those who are not?

In fact, over fifty years of psychological science have shown us that individual differences, attitudes, values and opinions have very little to do with broader trends in society's acceptance or rejection of diversity. Of course there are individuals who adopt extremist views, and the acts of these individuals are patently headline-grabbing. However, the notion that individuals with extreme racist views drive social change has been largely disproved by psychological science. Illustrating this is what is referred to as 'the authoritarian personality',[19] a theory that has been around since the 1950s. It was devised by the German sociologist Theodor Adorno as an attempt to understand the rise of fascism, World War Two and the Holocaust. The theory was heavily influenced by Freudian psychoanalytic principles and the idea that people have internal drives and impulses that have to be kept in check by the superego – which is essentially the representation of society via its laws, morals and norms. Prejudice arises, says the theory, as a defensive reaction against over-strict parenting methods. Having over-strict parents means that the child is unable to express any natural hostility towards those parents, and so transfers his or her aggression elsewhere (such as directing it at minority or low-status groups). These tendencies are then said to continue into adulthood, along with associated characteristics like an overly deferential attitude towards authority figures, who represent the parents.

Although intuitively appealing, personality theories like this are fundamentally flawed when we try to explain broad social trends. By definition, such theories aim to explain individual variation in attitudes and behaviours. They have difficulty accounting for widespread and uniform changes in attitudes towards other groups in society. For example, in the 1990s clear prejudice was witnessed in the former Yugoslavia, evident in its most extreme and brutal form – ethnic cleansing. Are we to conclude that a whole generation was raised in exactly the same way by authoritarian parents, and so all ended up with the same prejudiced and intolerant personalities? It's also the case that empirical evidence for individual personalities driving social change is hard to come by – or, indeed, disconfirms it. For instance, measures designed to identify people with authoritarian tendencies could not predict racism in South Africa in the 1950s – a culture in which prejudice was self-evident.

In sum, some people are bad people, but a few bad people can't account for social change. That some individuals have extreme racist or intolerant views cannot explain widespread problems that people have with diversity as a basic tenet of society. Nor can it explain established trends in attitudes towards diversity that reveal associations with significant social events such as the Holocaust, ethnic cleansing in the former Yugoslavia or apartheid in South Africa. Of course, racists may be encouraged to express their views openly under certain social conditions, like economic deprivation or terrorist threats, but this is a *reflection* of social change, not what drives it.

There is, however, an important lesson we can take from the authoritarian personality: the idea that minorities can be an easy target for the expression of displaced frustration and aggression. This is important because it illustrates the concept of *psychological threat*. Psychological threat is experienced on both conscious and subconscious levels and is constituted by anything that destabilises our view of the world. As I'll show in this book, stability and structure are essential goals of the human psyche. Threats to that stability make us behave in uniform and predictable ways. This basic idea – and it's supported by socio-demographic and historical evidence – suggests that shared social experiences may determine societal trends towards the rejection of diversity.

BOOM AND BUST: THE ECONOMICS OF INTOLERANCE

Humans react and adapt to their environment – I'm going to be talking a lot about this. The events we experience shape, focus and form the way we think. One clear manifestation of this is the well-documented relationship between economic depression and societal (in)tolerance of diversity. Put simply, the idea is that tension is caused by economic downturns which, in turn, produce aggressive impulses directed at vulnerable targets – minority groups – even when those groups bear no responsibility. It's kind of a less Freudian take on the authoritarian-personality idea – that pent-up frustration and aggression have to find an outlet somewhere. So rather than the aggression building in the subconscious and the frustration proving pivotal to the formation of one's personality, here the relationship is much more explicit. The economy is ruined and someone has to pay. Minority groups simply represent the path of least resistance.

Historical records support this idea. For instance, a correlation has been found between the price of cotton and lynchings of African Americans between 1882 and 1930.[20] As the price of cotton fell (indicating regional economic depression), lynchings rose. Two more recent illustrations: in the UK, government reports following the 2001 Bradford race riots suggested that poverty, deprivation and disillusionment were contributors; social and economic deprivation was also central to the events that led to the Yugoslav wars in the 1990s. And anthropological studies add further support: conflict has typically been found to be greater amongst tribes living in close proximity to one another and competing for locally hard-to-find resources like grazing land and water. In short, intergroup conflicts are often accompanied by competition for scarce resources. The more limited any given resource, the fiercer will be the competition.

This is pertinent, because since 2007 the world has experienced the worst economic depression for a generation. The relationship between economic hardship and intolerance found in historical records is emerging again before our eyes – and not just in political rhetoric about 'stemming the tide' of immigration, but also in the blatant racism of extremist political parties emerging all across Europe. Far-right groups capitalise on the tendency for people to scapegoat minorities in times of economic hardship, directing their frustration and anger over economic conditions. A striking example is the rise of Golden Dawn in Greece. This nationalist party gained 7 per cent of the vote in the 2012 elections, yet has been linked with numerous attacks on migrants and gay people. Across Europe the story is similar, from the French National Front (now the third-largest party) to Norway's Progress Party, to Italy's Lega Nord that has called for a limit to immigration from Muslim countries, to Austria's Freedom Party which won 20 per cent of the vote in the 2013 elections.

Extreme illustrations aside, what these trends suggest is that economic downturns trigger a generalised psychological 'closing of ranks' – a desire to be less inclusive, to preserve resources for those closest to us (for 'true' members of our group). This interpretation of archival and anthropological studies is backed up by evidence from behavioural science. In one classic 1970s study, white American airmen took part in a 'training exercise' with one white and one black co-worker.[21] What happened was that the experimenter fixed the outcome of the exercise so that the three-person team either succeeded or failed at the task. When the team succeeded, everyone was liked equally. When they failed, it was consistently the black co-worker who was blamed for the poor performance. This study mirrors the impact of economic recession on social attitudes towards diversity. When everything is going well, diversity is tolerated; but when resources become scarce, it's society's minorities who get the blame.

TERROR, EXISTENCE AND MORTALITY

On 11 September 2001, 3057 people were killed when four planes were hijacked by Al Qaeda terrorists, two of which were crashed into the twin towers of the World Trade Center in New York and one into the Pentagon in Washington DC. On 11 March 2004, a coordinated terrorist attack on the commuter train system in Madrid killed 192 and injured a further 2050 people. On the morning of 7 July 2005, four bombers killed themselves and fifty-two others when they exploded bombs on three Underground trains and a bus in central London.

Alongside the economic downturn, the rise of international terrorism is another shared experience that has come to define attitudes towards difference and diversity. Acts of terror destabilise and create uncertainty. In this they can be equated, psychologically, with the impact of economic recession. Accordingly, the relationship between Islamic terrorism and anti-Muslim sentiment parallels that observed for economic hardship. In fact, terrorism arguably constitutes an even greater psychological threat. Blame for economic troubles requires a mental leap, from generalised deprivation to the scapegoating of specific minorities. Terrorism strikes a deeper psychological chord, resonant in the essence of human mortality. Humans have a strong survival instinct. Unlike other animals, however, we also possess the intellectual capacity to realise that one day we will die. According to the social psychologist Jeff Greenberg and colleagues, this knowledge of our own impending mortality can cause 'existential terror'. Their terror-management theory claims that people adopt a range of religious beliefs, social norms and worldviews to 'manage' this terror.[22] Social systems, conventions and rules provide certainty and comfort to buffer our subconscious from this terror. Our cultures, and the view of the world they represent, are important because they allow us to transcend death, either literally through a belief in an afterlife, or symbolically, through lasting cultural achievements. They provide a sense of meaning, and help us maintain the belief that our lives are significant.

If cultural worldviews provide a sense of security, then reminding someone of his or her mortality should increase the need for that security, and therefore step up efforts to protect it from violation. Accordingly, behavioural studies show that religious intolerance increases immediately after people are asked to contemplate their own death. Acts of terror, by their nature, bring forth thoughts of one's own eventual death, which then trigger behaviours designed to bring certainty, structure and coherence back to one's world. From this perspective, it seems unsurprising that when constantly bombarded with images of terrorist attacks, people react by raising the societal drawbridge.

Diversity delivers uncertainty and instability, the opposite of what we need in order to counter the existential terror experienced when we're reminded of our own mortality.

SO WHERE DOES ALL THIS LEAVE DIVERSITY?

Despite the increase in extremism and the unravelling of public and political support for diversity, some studies paint a more positive picture of it. Evidence from socio-psychological research shows that when people *do* adopt multicultural ideologies, they promote greater tolerance and social integration. For instance, one study of multiculturalism was measured by asking participants to indicate the extent to which they believed that 'societal harmony is plausible to the degree that we recognise and appreciate the different, but equally valid, attributes of different ethnic groups'. In contrast, the degree of assimilation achieved was measured by asking participants to indicate the extent to which 'societal harmony is plausible to the degree that minority group members abandon their ethnic experience and adopt the ways of the mainstream American culture'. People who endorsed multiculturalism also endorsed affirmative-action policies, were less concerned about immigration, and supported a flexible English-speaking policy that allowed bilingual classrooms.

If diversity can have positive effects, why then isn't it adopted wholesale? The problem rests with the prevailing social climate. As we saw earlier, economic recession, terrorism – indeed, anything that poses a threat, whether realistic or symbolic – triggers people's negative reactions to diversity. Recent research has confirmed this direct relationship between threat and the distrust of multiculturalism.[23] It assessed how strongly white Americans identified as white American, before exposing them to multicultural policy statements. It emerged that strongly identifying white Americans, exposed to multiculturalism, subsequently reported a greater desire to maintain hierarchical relations amongst groups as well as more prejudice towards minorities. The researchers also found that participants exposed to multicultural policy statements were less willing to allocate campus funds to organisations promoting diversity – but this applied only to those white Americans who strongly identified as such.

This can be explained by the concept of psychological threat. Specifically, because multicultural ideology rests on the appreciation of different identities, it could be that the white Americans in this study felt that the values of their group were being jeopardised. In other words, multiculturalism may trigger a threat to the group's values, which has been shown to increase intergroup discord. Even words associated with multiculturalism can be perceived as threatening. In a related study, participants were presented with words associated with multiculturalism (such as 'difference', 'diversity') and with assimilation ('colour-blindness', 'sameness'). The white participants showed a significant bias towards pairing multiculturalism with notions of social exclusion, and colour-blindness with notions of social inclusion, whereas no such difference emerged as far as minorities were concerned.

In sum, while research has shown that promoting multi-cultural ideologies generally leads to greater tolerance, empathy, understanding and perspective-taking amongst majority-group members, as well as greater engagement and social inclusion amongst those belonging to minority groups, majorities appear compelled to reject multicultural ideology when it is seen as a threat to their higher social status.

SUMMARY

In this chapter I've introduced an idea that lies at the heart of this book: that to fully understand the impact of social and cultural diversity on our communities we must look beyond the political to the *psychological*. This notion can be traced right back to the origins of psychology as a science, and it's one that resonates in modern-day research. However I showed that understanding dissatisfaction with diversity is not about individuals, but about shared social experiences. Archival accounts reveal a significant relationship: economic downturns and terror attacks correlate with hate crimes, prejudice and anti-immigration sentiment. I've argued that our brains interpret these events as threats to a core need for certainty and structure. Under these conditions our psychologies reject diversity – which by its nature introduces instability into our social ecologies.

This is quite depressing for anyone who believes in a world where we can all just get along together, where difference is celebrated and diversity is a defining feature of everyday life. So what exactly is it about diversity that people can't get on with? To answer this question we need to understand the fundamental function of the human mind. In the next chapter I'll explore the mind's most basic drive, the principle that lies at the heart of all of our behaviour and that helps us understand why people are so compelled to reject diversity and difference.

CHAPTER 2

THE PREDICTION MACHINE

We humans need things to make sense. It's one of our defining characteristics, driving discoveries in fields like chemistry, medicine and mechanics. It fires the imagination and encourages exploration; it has fuelled generation upon generation of scientists seeking to solve the mysteries of the world around us.

This need for things to make sense is innate – evolved, honed and eventually hardwired through the course of human history. We've developed a number of innate drives that have proven, over millennia, to be adaptive for our survival (that is, which have enabled us to thrive and survive in the environments we find ourselves in). The urge to procreate and to protect our offspring are behaviours that are hardwired because they ensure the survival of the species. In the same way, as a species we have evolved a drive to make sense of the world – a preference for predictability. Predictability enables planning, and it helps us build and grow. For instance, being able to predict which animals we could eat and which would eat us meant that our ancestors could navigate the world safely – and live long enough, as well as being healthy enough, to pass on their genes. We are, in essence, prediction machines.

Our brains have evolved to ensure our protection and survival, and to survive we need to predict. After basic physiological needs – air, water, food, sleep, sex – the psychological need for stability, structure and security comes next, and is pivotal to predicting our behaviour. Think about the major life goals we strive towards: financial stability, personal security, health. We take out insurance policies to counter uncertainty in all of these areas. Achieving stability, structure and security is arguably the single most important psychological drive we have.

Have you ever looked up at the sky and seen something familiar in the clouds? That's the brain looking for patterns. It never stops, constantly generating theories, predictions and projections. In the 1950s Fritz Heider, an Austrian psychologist, was the first to really pin down the importance of a predictable world for the human mind. Heider recognised as a fundamental part of our psyche this core drive towards achieving stability and our need to predict and control. Many of the behaviours we exhibit, he argued, can ultimately be traced back to this need and to the mental processes we engage to reduce uncertainty. Most importantly, he stated that in this quest we engage the 'naive' scientific mind that resides within all of us, one that constantly stands ready to explore, examine, extrapolate and infer.

THE SCIENTIST

We can solve complex mathematical problems, use sophisticated logic to construct arguments; we can be cogent, balanced and analytical. Heider believed we apply these scientific skills in everyday thinking; that just like real scientists, we act like the naive scientist in our attempts to understand the world. Heider's thinking spawned several decades of work testing this hypothesis. Elaborate theories were created to specify how our naive scientific minds apply clear logic to understand everyday events. One approach, Attribution Theory, dominated the field for decades. It was an attempt to describe and explain how people attribute causality to other people's actions. So imagine you arrive home to find your partner embroiled in a heated argument with your neighbour . . . how do you make sense of this? Well, according to Attribution Theory[24] you'd analyse three types of information, referred to as consensus, consistency and distinctiveness information.

Consensus information is the extent to which other people in the scene react in the same way as the target person (in this case your partner). So is your partner the only one who argues with your neighbour, or do other people generally argue with him too?

Consistency information is the extent to which the target person reacts in the same way on different occasions. So in this case, does your partner always argue with your neighbour, or is their relationship usually pretty good?

Distinctiveness information is the extent to which the target person reacts in the same way in other social contexts. So does your partner argue only with your neighbour, or with everyone?

These three types of information are then combined in a complex way to generate possible explanations for the altercation. The presence of consensus information (i.e., everyone else behaves in the same way as your partner) implies a situational cause. In other words, the cause can be found within the situation in which your partner finds him or herself. In contrast, the absence of consensus information implies a dispositional, or personality-based, cause. The presence of consistency information (your partner behaves in the same way all the time) implies a dispositional cause, while the absence of consistency information implies a situational cause. The presence of distinctiveness information (your partner acts in the same way in many different situations) implies a dispositional cause, but the absence of distinctiveness information implies a situational cause.

According to this model, when you're observing someone's behaviour in a particular social context it's the combined impact of these three types of information that will determine what type of conclusion you draw. So if your partner rarely argues with other people (distinctiveness is low) and everyone argues with your neighbour (consensus is high), this implies that your neighbour is argumentative. If consistency information is also high – your neighbour is always arguing with your partner – then all the sources of information converge, leading to the conclusion that your neighbour is argumentative. However, if consistency is low – your neighbour rarely argues with your partner – or either consensus or distinctiveness does not accord with consistency, coming to a conclusion is more difficult and the naive scientist will need to weigh up the three types of information more carefully in order to arrive at a the cause of your partner's behaviour.

Are you lost yet? If you are, then relax – you're human. We really *don't* think like this. OK, yes, if you get a bunch of behavioural scientists together and ask them to analyse precisely how people make sense of the world, they'll come up with something like this – and that's exactly what they did with

Attribution Theory. But most people just don't have the time, the inclination or the scientific training to engage in this sort of complex way of thinking.

If, however, we're not naive scientists, then what are we? The answer is that, wherever possible, we're 'cognitive misers'.

THE MISER

The trouble with an irrepressible need to predict the future is that the future is just too darn difficult to predict. As the scene featuring our quarrelsome neighbour illustrates, the amount of information needed to accurately assess situations and predict future behaviours is considerable. The brain can't cope with all this, especially considering we typically engage in hundreds of social interactions each and every day. It's exhausting, and to cope the brain needs a strategy – one that will facilitate the acquisition of answers with minimal mental effort. It needs to rely on something else. It needs to rely on gut instinct.

The only problem with this is that it can send us barking wildly up the wrong tree. To illustrate, here's a classic study from the 1960s, carried out at the height of the Cold War.[25] Each participant was instructed to read an essay written by a fellow student. The essays contained arguments supporting Fidel Castro's rule in Cuba – something that would have been incredibly bold in 1960s America. However, the participants were also given a crucial piece of information: namely, that the writers had been instructed, by the experimenter, to write pro Castro. The participants were then asked to guess the real attitudes of the writers towards Castro.

OK, so imagine yourself as a participant in this study, at that time. Everybody (pretty much) is anti-Castro. With the Cuban

Missile Crisis and everything else going on, he's the most significant threat to your existence you can imagine. And you know that the writer whose essay you are about to read has been told to write a pro-Castro message. Now, do you think the writer is pro- or anti-Castro?

Incredibly, the participants utterly failed to take the discounting information into account, and on the whole concluded that the writer *was* pro-Castro. In other words, the most accessible information lying there before them was just too tempting. This is what the cognitive miser is all about – taking the easiest route to the answer without expending too much mental effort. Yes, they could have discounted the essay on the basis of knowing that each writer had been told to write a pro-Castro essay, but where would this have left them? Still none the wiser about the writer's attitude, still uncertain. That the only piece of evidence they had – the essay – was flawed didn't matter. After all, it still could have reflected the writer's opinion.

What does this study illustrate? That in the end the brain will settle for an answer, any answer, that removes uncertainty. Accuracy plays second fiddle to the need to be certain. We are, to quote the Princeton psychologist Susan Fiske, 'cognitive misers'. We desperately want answers, but don't have the time or ability to engage in complex attributional calculations. Instead we look for probable cause, clues and possible answers, something salient that offers a 'good enough' explanation.

We don't even know we're doing it. Here's another classic judgement bias that skews people's responses. This one's known as 'anchoring', which is the tendency to give answers that are delimited by, or anchored to, a starting quantity that is given. In another Cold War study[26] half the participants were asked whether they thought there was a 'greater or less than 1 per cent chance' of a nuclear war occurring (in scientific terms this is called 'condition 1') and the other half were asked whether they thought there was a 'greater or less than 90 per cent chance' of a nuclear war (in scientific terms this comparison group is called 'condition 2'). Afterwards they were asked to follow up and give a numeric estimate. This question was identical in both conditions, so surely the answer should have been the same regardless of which question?

Not so! The 'anchor' in the question had a huge impact on the answer people gave. Participants who were asked the 1 per cent question estimated a 10 per cent chance of a nuclear war occurring, while those who were asked the 90 per cent question estimated a 25 per cent chance. No one realised the effect of the anchors.

Similar effects abound in behavioural science. In studies of decision-making by juries it has been shown that when first asked to consider a harsh verdict, people are subsequently harsher in their final decision, compared with when they first consider a lenient verdict. Again, our need for certainty outstrips our need for accuracy or veracity as our number 1 goal; it makes obvious answers feel right – even though they're affected, and predicted, by irrelevant and extraneous influences.

We crave information – regardless of whether it's significant or useful. The simplest of cues can play havoc with our heads, and even our hearts. In a famous study of interpersonal attraction[27] an attractive female researcher asked a group of men to carry out some psychological tests atop the 230-foot Capilano Canyon Suspension Bridge in Canada and compared their responses with a group who did the same but on a much lower and more secure bridge. The findings revealed that the men who completed the tests on the swaying suspension bridge were more likely to call the attractive researcher later on for further details of the study.

Further details? Yeah, OK.

Heart palpitations, shortness of breath, nausea and muscle weakness . . . these are reactions one might feel when anxious – such as when on a swaying 230-foot bridge – but also when sexually aroused. In this study the men misattributed their physiological fear response, caused by the swaying bridge, to sexual attraction for the female researcher.

Beyond the frivolity and fun of courtship rituals, this insatiable need to feel certain can have devastating consequences. In the 1986 space shuttle Challenger disaster seven astronauts were killed when, seventy-three seconds after take-off, the shuttle exploded. The subsequent inquiry determined that the primary cause of the accident was a rubber ring joining two sections of the rocket together. Because the joint was not properly sealed, rocket fuel escaped and ignited, causing the explosion. The inquiry concluded that the decision-making process preceding the launch was severely flawed. Specifically, the day before the launch, engineers were concerned about the cold weather, arguing that the rubber rings had never been tested at such low temperatures. NASA officials were, however, sceptical and urged them to reconsider. Rather than sticking to their position, the engineers changed their minds, agreeing that the shuttle was ready to launch. The flight had already been delayed several times and the agency was worried that the American public would start to lose faith in them. The result was a catastrophic accident. The human flaws that defined this disaster illustrate what psychologists have called 'groupthink' – the tendency for groups to feel an excessive pressure to reach consensus. Yet another manifestation of our relentless need for certainty, especially under pressure, and at the high cost of accuracy.

In sum, the cognitive miser is neither willing nor able to devote the mental energy necessary to think like the naive scientist. Instead, we latch onto the most obvious cue to make our decision – because it provides a 'good enough' answer and, most importantly, satisfies the need to reduce uncertainty. Our brain's desire to take short-cuts compels us to make quick and easy but erroneous decisions. By and large these short-cuts are whatever feels right at the time – whatever most easily comes to mind or grabs our attention. On the one hand this strategy makes perfect sense for a brain that needs to manage, process and act upon a huge amount of information. On the other, as we've seen, it can lead to decisions with profound and life-threatening consequences. Cognitive misers seek sense in whatever form they can, so as to maintain the 'happy illusion' of a certain and predictable world.

THE HAPPY ILLUSION

The overriding need for the brain to construct a positive, predictable illusion of reality is exemplified in the Just World Fallacy. This is a name for another predictability bias that reveals how happy we humans are to settle for certainty over accuracy – a happy illusion that the world is as it should be, and makes sense.

The Just World Fallacy captures the essence of the sense-seeker's happy illusion: it describes a tendency for people to always assume that a person's actions bring about fair and just consequences for him or her. Consistent with this idea are studies that have shown how believing in a just world leads to greater life satisfaction and well-being and less depression. It buffers us from the reality that the world is unpredictable, and protects us from the stress that uncertainty brings. It's a little like karma: good acts will, eventually, lead to good outcomes for the individual, and evil is eventually punished, whether in this world or the next. It is a bias that fundamentally sums up our blinding drive to preserve stability, justice and a sense of order – the world is fair and people get what they deserve.

A famous illustration can be found in Stanley Milgram's studies of obedience,[28] carried out at Yale in the 1960s. Milgram was interested in what aspects of the human psyche could possibly have allowed people to commit such terrible atrocities in World War Two. In particular, he was interested in what made Nazi guards obey orders that would lead them to commit horrendous acts of violence against the Jews. Milgram thought not that a whole nation of people could be inherently evil, but rather that there might be conditions under which anyone might abandon his or her own sense of right and wrong.

Milgram's experiment went like this. Those taking part were told that the study concerned the effects of punishment (negative reinforcement) on learning. A participant entered the laboratory ostensibly with a second participant apparently just like himself, but who was actually in league with the experimenter. The experimenter then allocated them a role each, apparently quite randomly but in fact set up so that the real participant was always the 'teacher' and the experimenter's confederate always the 'learner'. The task for the learner was to learn word pairs. Each time he made a mistake he was supposedly given an electric shock by the teacher. The intensity of the shock appeared to increase each time the learner made a mistake. The confederate then explained that he was fifty years old and had a heart problem. However, the experimenter dismissed this and strapped him into the waiting chair, attaching the electrodes that would apparently deliver the shocks. At this stage the learner received a real 15-volt shock from these electrodes to enhance the realism, but none of the subsequent shocks were real.

The confederate/learner was in a different room from the real participant, answering questions through an intercom. The participant asked the questions, recorded whether the answer was correct or incorrect, and administered the (supposed) electric shock if an incorrect answer was given. At any query the experimenter simply said, 'Please continue' – this was scripted so that each participant received the same response from the experimenter. During the course of the task the confederate made several deliberate mistakes. The script ensured experimental control: all participants were exposed to precisely the same situation. At 150 volts the learner demanded to be released, shouting: 'Experimenter! That's enough! Get me out of here . . . My heart's starting to bother me now. I refuse to go on!' At 180 volts the learner shouted that he could no longer stand the pain. At 300 he refused to give any more answers – which the experimenter said to simply treat as incorrect answers. There were screams of agony at each subsequent shock, and then from 330 volts onwards, silence. The last switch was labelled '450 volts: XXX – danger, severe shock'.

Looking at this script one cannot imagine participants continuing to administer shocks, given the protests and the apparent medical emergency that ensued at 300 volts. Milgram wanted to confirm the expectation that 'reasonable' people would refuse to obey such apparently irresponsible orders. Before the experiment he had obtained predictions from college students, older middle-class people and psychiatrists. All of these groups predicted that all the participants would refuse to continue well before the 450-volt limit. In fact the psychiatrists predicted that only 0.1 per cent would obey the experimenter completely; such behaviour, should it happen, would surely indicate some sort of mental problem that one would expect in only a tiny proportion of the population.

What Milgram actually found in this experiment was astonishing. He observed a huge discrepancy between what people expected to find and how the participants actually responded to the experimenter's orders. At 210 volts everyone had predicted that most of the participants, 86 per cent, would refuse to go on – this is well after the learner has complained about his heart and shouted out in agony. In fact, at 210 volts not a single participant had defected. After this point some did begin to question the experimenter, but only a tiny minority. At 315 volts 96 per cent of people should have defected, but only 22.5 per cent had done so. At this point the learner was screaming at each shock. Overall, 24 out of 30 obeyed the experimenter right up to the maximum 450-volts switch labelled 'XXX – danger, severe shock'.

Milgram's findings caused quite a stir, and a debate that continues today. Were people really so savage that they would happily engage in apparently immoral acts, just because they were being told to do so by someone else? The findings raised issues that cut to the core of human nature. Could so many people be willing to do serious harm to an innocent person?

The answer was yes they can, and do – and did – all, arguably, in the service of making sense of the situation.

Put yourself in the unenviable position of one of Milgram's participants. What are you supposed to do? On the one hand you're apparently administering visceral pain to an innocent victim (whose only 'crime' is to have allowed himself to be randomly chosen as 'the learner'). Surely you should stop what you're doing. But on the other hand, you're in a highly respectable setting (Yale University) and here's a respectable scientist giving you clear orders as if there's nothing at all odd about such a crazy situation. What should you do? Here the cognitive miser takes over – don't rock the boat, take the easiest course, the line of least resistance: obey, it must be OK, it must make sense.

So people need things to make sense, and they're willing to overlook all sorts of moral or logical ambiguities to achieve this. But Milgram's studies show something else too: the importance of social pressure. In these experiments it was Milgram the reputed scientist, in the high-status setting, that provided the short-cut to certainty. Relying on social cues makes a lot of sense for the cognitive miser; as we'll see in the unfolding chapters, it is people and social situations that have proven pivotal in shaping the human mind. We understand the world through our relations with others, by observing others' actions and reactions. People provide predictability, a sense of belonging and a sense of stability to our lives. Unsurprisingly, if you mess with people's sense of belonging, you mess with their sense of safety, stability and security. Belonging is key to the cognitive miser's pursuit of predictability, certainty and meaning.

SUMMARY

In this chapter I've mapped out some fundamental principles of human thinking and described how our brains are, in essence, prediction machines. That's what both the naive scientist and the cognitive miser are really all about: predicting the behaviour of others. It's not that one way of thinking is better than the other. The naive scientist is accurate but this approach takes time and effort and steals our attention from other potentially important tasks. The cognitive miser is quick and efficient, but less accurate. Both systems of thought lead to the same outcome, only they reach it in different ways depending upon the immediate goals and the state of the person making the decision. The point is that both systems are designed to do one thing: predict the future.

Think about it, what's the ultimate goal of any decision we make? Whether short term (deciding what to have for dinner) or long term (saving for retirement), everything we do is designed to set us up for dealing with the future. We imagine different futures so as to enable us to build models for the future that may then become rules, norms and expectations.

That our brains are prediction machines makes perfect sense. What does an organism need to do the best to survive? Predict the future. Our ancestors needed to learn quickly which types of animals to avoid and which would make a great meal. They needed to know what landscape characteristics were most conducive to staying alive. Being next to a river is great for water supply in the short term, but if it floods in winter this adds to the challenge. Building a camp both near water but on high ground will best ensure survival. It is this evolutionary basis for the human brain's ability to predict the future that suggests it is a core component shaping everything we do.

More problematically, it is also absolutely central to how people react to diversity, to their attitudes towards difference and to their prejudices towards others. It is to how people perceive and process such differences that I turn next.

CHAPTER 3

A WORLD OF DIFFERENCE

The human ability to categorise is quintessentially a way of achieving stability, structure and predictability. It is a way of classifying any collection of things – objects, events, opinions, attitudes, concepts – that provides maximal information about them with minimal effort. It enables us to label a group of things as being all related to each other in some way, all interconnected to a greater or lesser extent (for instance, dogs, furniture, weather, cheese, vegetables, Manchester United), and to compare one thing with another (British versus French, dogs versus cats, rock versus pop and so on).

The extent to which a category member is typical of that category is the extent to which it is easy to bring to mind. Think for a moment about an item of fruit. I bet most of you thought of an apple or an orange. I'm pretty certain you didn't think of a kiwi fruit, and almost certainly not of a tomato. Apples and oranges are highly typical of the category 'fruit' and are easy to bring to mind. In contrast, kiwi fruit and tomatoes, while still members of the fruit category, are quite atypical, and so are brought to mind far less easily. Categorisation is not just useful – it is essential to the organisation of knowledge. The brain could not cope with remembering every single item of fruit that it had ever encountered, so it abstracts key features and stores this generalised, simplified representation. The abstract representation comprises mainly those attributes most commonly encountered; those that have become the typical examples of the category.

This is important because, from the brain's point of view, people can be categorised just like any object, event, concept or idea. For social categories, typical members are what we think of as social stereotypes. For instance, the typical member of the 'mechanic' category is a man, which may lead to errors in categorising when we encounter a woman doing the same job. We'll get back to stereotypes a little later on, but for now the important thing is that the cognitive miser uses categorisation as the ultimate short-cut – a way of assigning meaning, structure and predictability to the world around her or him.

So social categorisation is one of the fundamental truths of social reality. When we categorise we clarify and refine our perception of the world. Categorising provides the meaning and sense of certainty we crave; it helps us to predict social behaviour and provides prescriptive norms for understanding ourselves in relation to others. This fundamental role of social categorisation was revealed most clearly in a series of experiments carried out in Bristol in the 1970s by the social psychologist Henri Tajfel.

THE MERE CATEGORISATION EFFECT

Tajfel wanted to understand the psychology of prejudice. He was highly influenced by his experiences as a Polish Jew in World War Two and by the fact that something as seemingly innocuous as a social categorisation – in his case, as a Jew – could be used to justify such horrific acts of violence and aggression. His drive to understand how categorisation could underlie such atrocities led him to develop what have become some of the most important and influential studies in social psychology.

Tajfel developed an experimental technique called the Minimal Group Paradigm. The MGP creates an artificial basis for categorisation. In Tajfel's original experiments[29] the participants, schoolchildren, were first asked which of a selection of abstract paintings they preferred. On the basis of their responses, each participant was then allocated to either the Klee or the Kandinsky group, ostensibly depending on whether they had shown a preference for the paintings of Paul Klee or those of Wassily Kandinsky. This is what the experimenter told the participants, but the allocation to groups was in fact completely random. The participants then completed a task in which they were required to allocate points (via code numbers) to people in the two groups. The points were allocated using a series of decision matrices (numerical tables) on which the participants indicated, with a cross in one column, how much each member of their own group – the 'ingroup' – and of the other group – the 'outgroup' – should receive. Importantly, the allocation of points to individuals was anonymous, or they might have recognised their friends and given them more points. All that distinguished people was a random code number (e.g. person number 419) and their group membership (Klee or Kandinsky).

What Tajfel found was a persistent tendency for participants to allocate more points to people in their own group than to those in the other. At first glance this might not seem surprising. It's human nature, right? Just competition. But take a moment to think what this study really says about human nature. There was absolutely no justifiable reason to give more points to one group than to the other. There could be no self-interest: the participant would receive no money, nor would he or she 'win' the game either as an individual or as a member of his or her group. It was anonymous – they knew nothing about the people receiving the points other than that they were in one group rather than the other. To the naive scientist this should make no sense whatsoever – responses to this task should be absolutely random.

But of course, we're not just naive scientists. We're also cognitive misers: we're compelled to look for patterns, to impose order on ambiguous situations. This is exactly what Tajfel's studies show in regard to social categorisation. The participants are placed in a bizarre context, asked to allocate points with no instruction, guidelines or explanation. So as cognitive misers they impose order: they allocate more points to one group than to the other. I remember doing these studies myself as a PhD student. Like Tajfel, I didn't think I'd find an effect and so I was struck by the results. Time and again, people with no logical justification whatsoever preferred people who shared their own minimal group label (even simply 'A') over someone who had been given another minimal group label (even simply 'B').

The MGP offers further insight into humans' powerful desire to create a predictable world. Tajfel gave the participants different versions of the matrices used to award points to each other. Importantly, these matrices assessed different allocation strategies. The choices made in the Minimal Group Paradigm reveal a consistent tendency to choose maximum differentiation rather than maximal ingroup profit. In other words, it was more important to the participants to differentiate the two groups from each other in the study, by awarding more points to one than to the other, than to maximise the total number of points allocated to their own group.

This finding, that people would sacrifice self-gain just to make their group seem more different from an opposing group, shows that the primary motivation driving behaviour here is the desire to impose structure, to reduce uncertainty. The driver of the participants' choices was the desire to create a meaningful difference between 'us' and 'them'. Doing so has the advantage of simplifying things so that information about people in the immediate context can be more efficiently processed, enabling judgements to be made with little effort. In the MGP the participants are given so little information that their drive to differentiate is thrown into sharp focus. The only way structure can be achieved is by allocating more points to one group than to the other.

This mere-categorisation effect has been replicated many times and using many different ways to categorise people and many different measures. The importance of this finding lies in the fact that it suggests there's a psychological component to prejudice, beyond any economic, political or historical factor. Unlike real social groups defined by nationality, religion or age, here there was no known economic imbalance, no known political motivation, no past interaction, not even a substantive meaning ascribed to the groups. This most basic form of categorisation reveals that categories are fundamentally functional and used spontaneously to define the social contexts we find ourselves in. The MGP demonstrates the human brain as a prediction machine at work: motivated to make the world as simple, structured and easy to predict as possible.

This tendency is at its most heinous in what psychologists call 'infrahumanisation'. 'Infrahumanisation' is concerned with how we attribute emotion to other people. Primary emotions are feelings that both humans and animals are perceived to experience, such as *joy*, *surprise*, *fright* and *sadness*. Secondary emotions – *admiration*, *hope*, *indignation*, *melancholy* – are more complex and are thought of as uniquely human; critically, they are used to distinguish humans from animals. Infrahumanisation is the specific tendency to attribute the uniquely human secondary emotions to outgroup members to a lesser extent than to ingroup members. Put another way, it is the tendency people have to assign only primary emotions, but not secondary emotions, to outgroups. This is a manifestation of categorisation bias, enabling people to see outgroups as less than human and thus justifying violence and aggression towards them in the same way that such people consider it justifiable to kill animals. For instance, some research has found that French-speaking Belgians more strongly associated French-speaking Belgian (ingroup) names with uniquely human secondary emotions than they did North African (outgroup) names, which they associated more closely with primary emotions (which were not uniquely human).

Some quite shocking consequences of infrahumanisation have been uncovered. In August 2005, Hurricane Katrina flooded 80 per cent of New Orleans and claimed over 1800 victims, leaving around 60,000 residents homeless. In one study,[30] White, Black and Latino Americans were told a fictional news story about a mother who had lost a child during the hurricane. When they were asked which emotions they thought the mother would be feeling, some of the participants said they thought she would have experienced fewer secondary emotions if she was an outgroup member than if she was an ingroup member. Furthermore, those that did not show such infrahumanisation said they would volunteer for the relief effort.

Such research supports the idea that infrahumanisation boils down to thinking about the human–animal divide. If outgroups are perceived as less than human – that is, dehumanised – then expressing aggression towards them is made easier. And the wider people perceive the human–animal divide, the greater the prejudice observed towards immigrants.[31]

MAKING SENSE OF MIGRANTS

What does all this mean for diversity, multiculturalism and attitudes towards immigration? The studies I've discussed give us a glimpse of the human mind in full prediction machine mode – using short-cuts, categories and abstractions to make sense of the world. Categorisation, as one of our most powerful cognitive tools, is of particular use in our attempts to structure that world. However, the drive to create certainty, clarity and meaning has a critical consequence for modern society: because multiculturalism and diversity are by their very nature antithetical to the human desire for simplicity and structure. Far from creating clarity, a diverse society introduces ambiguity. A hundred years ago British pretty much meant white + Christian; now British means white, black, Asian, Christian, Muslim, Sikh ... How can categories be used to predict behaviour in diverse societies, where differentiation between one category and another is confused and cross-cutting? Who is *us* and who is *them*? A brain intent on creating a predictable world will resist diversity to protect its sense of stability, structure and security.

With my colleagues Mark Rubin and Stefania Paolini I've carried out experiments demonstrating how this need for clarity directly impacts on people's perceptions of migrants. We tested the idea that migrants will be liked less than non-migrants because of this fundamental preference, even at a highly abstract level.

In our study[32] we split a group of undergraduate students into two groups: A and B. We then asked a few members of the A group to join the B group, and a few of the B group to join the A group. The ones who moved represented social migrants. When it came to asking people to say how much they liked each of the individuals in the groups, on average they liked those who had migrated less than those who hadn't.

Very much like Tajfel's original MGP, this is a completely abstract task. The groups were called A and B. Membership of the groups was totally random. There was no possible economic, political, cultural (or logical) reason why anyone should like anyone in these groups more than anyone else. However, on average participants still liked those who had not migrated more than those who had. Simply moving from one category to another was enough, in relative terms, to be disliked. In other words, there was a basic cognitive bias against migrants.

We also asked those taking part how difficult they found it to think about the 'migrants' and about the people who had remained in their original A or B group. The migrants were reported as being harder to think about, supporting the notion that they were liked less than non-migrants because they were more difficult to process, to categorise. For the cognitive miser, it seems, migrants simply 'do not compute'. On a fundamental level, all this suggests that people find it easier to think about Britons in Britain, Norwegians in Norway and Algerians in Algeria than any other combination of nationality and nation. Diversity seems just too difficult to parse for a mind irrepressibly intent on establishing certainty, clarity, stability and structure.

So far I've offered evidence supporting the notion that the human brain is a prediction machine, and implied that this is because from an evolutionary standpoint an organism that can predict its environment will be much better able to survive and therefore pass on its genes to successive generations. This evolutionary argument lies at the core of the argument I'm making in this book, so that's what we'll turn to next.

THE INGROUP TRIBE

Darwinian principles of evolution provide a powerful guide for psychologists in their quest to understand human behaviour. Evolutionary psychologists have shown that the tendency to reject difference and diversity derives from our ancestral past. They argue that one of the most significant threats to safety in human history came from hostile outgroups, and that this fear remains programmed in the modern mind. Accordingly, they claim many psychological processes have evolved to protect us from the potential threat posed by outgroups. Proponents of this perspective argue that evolved human preferences for stability, simplicity and structure reflect behavioural adaptations that conferred a survival advantage to humans in the distant past. These preferences are exemplified in the way we

mentally represent groups and group differences to ourselves.
In other words, a manifestation of the brain's need for simplicity and structure is our inclination to categorise, generalise,
stereotype and differentiate people from different cultural
groups than our own.

Evolutionary social psychologists argue that many of the
behavioural tendencies we observe in modern humans are a
response to environmental adaptations that faced our ancestors.
The reasoning is that humans have evolved so rapidly over the
last hundred thousand years that our cognitive systems and
behavioural tendencies are catching up with modern society
and civilisation. According to this view, social cognition
(thinking about people and our relationships with them) and
social behaviour (such as prejudice, conflict, leadership
and cooperation) are also adaptations to the social world that
our ancestors had to negotiate to survive. So in humans' ancestral habitats one of the most significant survival threats came
not from tigers, snakes or spiders, but from bands of other
humans. Hostile outgroup members were in competition for
the same scarce natural resources – food, fuel and shelter – and
inevitably conflicts would occur. Thus, goes the argument, our
ancestors evolved to be so highly attuned to outgroup threats
that this mechanism has become a fixture in the human brain.

Recall the discussion of categorisation processes outlined
earlier. Social categorisation occurs because it confers simplicity and structure onto a chaotic world; it enables prediction,
and prediction aids survival. Evolutionary psychology provides
a specific reason why simplifying our world into categories
offers an evolutionary advantage: it enabled our ancestors to
rapidly distinguish friend from foe, 'us' from 'them', and in so

doing helped them to more efficiently activate an appropriate fight-or-flight response.

For instance, a major survival challenge in ancestral environments was the need to avoid communicable pathogens and parasites. Individuals would have been more likely to possess antibodies to the pathogens transmitted by fellow ingroup members than to those transmitted by outgroup members. Thus outgroups posed a greater risk of transmitting disease. Interestingly, there is evidence that pregnant women today exhibit both a preference for the company of ingroup members and avoidance of outgroup members during the first trimester, when both the foetus and the mother are most susceptible to infection. In a similar vein, ethnocentric attitudes have been found to correlate positively with individuals' perceived vulnerability to disease.

The mechanisms that facilitate ingroup bias in the Minimal Group Paradigm can therefore be understood as having evolved to avoid potential danger posed by outgroups. Indeed, research has demonstrated that when people find themselves in situations that make them feel vulnerable, they are more likely to rely on stereotypes. For instance, for a species that relies on vision to successfully navigate landscapes and avoid any associated dangers, darkness can connote vulnerability to potential harm. Accordingly, it has been found that a dark as opposed to a well-lit room amplifies the association between an individual's belief in a dangerous world and his or her distrust of outgroups.

PREDICTION AND THREAT

According to the evolutionary perspective that I've just described, prejudice is a manifestation of a hardwired propensity to predict threat in one's social environment. Our tendency to avoid potentially threatening outgroups is demonstrated time and time again in modern social-psychology experiments. For instance, one of the most basic mechanisms designed to help us learn about our environments is what's referred to as 'associative learning'. In essence, the more we see two things occurring at the same time, the more we learn to predict that one will follow the other.

You'll probably have heard of Pavlov's Dog and the studies that show a dog salivates on hearing a bell that has previously been repeatedly paired with the delivery of food. Well, the same basic mechanism can be seen in human learning about groups. In a now classic learning study,[33] researchers presented participants with pairings of the national-category label 'Dutch' with negative words and the national-category label 'Swedish' with positive words. They found that in the former case the subsequent evaluation of Dutch people was more negative than the evaluation of Swedes. However, when Dutch was paired with positive words and Swedish with negative words, the opposite occurred. In other words, it appeared that the repeated association of Dutch with positivity led to a more positive evaluation of this group – a case of the human brain learning through association.

Other research has shown that we register people's group membership within milliseconds of meeting them – in ancestral habitats, an essential way of distinguishing friend from foe. In modern terms, when people are asked to think about aversive scenarios they display greater support for the ideology espoused by their own governments and more bias against others.

If the learning principles outlined above apply, we should automatically think of more positive associations with ingroup names and negative associations with outgroup names. The strength of these associative links can be measured using response times to lexical decision tasks (i.e., tasks involving the allocation of different words to categories). For example, if positive words are associated with ingroup-related words (such as, for nationality, names like Pierre, Nikita, Brad), then the one should facilitate the response time to the other. That's to say, identifying a positive word as positive should be quicker when the word preceding it is also one with positive connotations. If ingroup, but not outgroup, words speed up responses to positive words, the implication is that ingroup, but not outgroup, words are associatively positive. Generic ingroup and outgroup designators show this effect. For instance, research has shown that priming an individual with the word 'we' led to faster response times in identifying subsequent positive words as positive than did the word 'they'.

One of the most frequently used measures of implicit attitude is the Implicit Association Test (IAT). This is a task that identifies the speed with which participants can categorise positive or negative stimuli (e.g., positive or negative words) alongside ingroup or outgroup stimuli (e.g., names or faces). It typically shows that people have an implicit ingroup-favouring bias. Specifically, people find it easier to associate their own group with positive words and the outgroup with negative words. The IAT has been used to reveal bias against a whole range of groups, from women to Muslims to older people.

So why do we so readily learn these category-based associations? It is because, according to evolutionary psychologists, one of the most significant threats to our ancestors' safety came from hostile outgroup members. As such, many psychological processes have been developed to protect us from this potential

threat. Proponents of this perspective argue that evolved preferences for homogeneity, stability, simplicity and structure
reflect behavioural adaptations that conferred a survival advantage in the distant past. In keeping with this view, human social
cognition has adapted to ancestral environments as defined by
simple us-versus-them category boundaries, providing a clear
way of distinguishing friend from foe. This preference for
representing the world using categorical differences is reflected
in contemporary social-psychological research.

Even stronger support comes from research in social neuroscience. While the behavioural evidence of the kind of evolved
systems described here is open to alternative explanations such
as social learning, brain structures and systems that react in
ways consistent with evolutionary principles are harder to
question. Social-neuroscience research aims to identify brain
structures that are functionally associated with particular
thoughts or behaviours. Notable here is a study by Elizabeth
Phelps and colleagues,[34] who used Functional Magnetic
Resonance Imaging (fMRI) to examine which brain structures
are associated with the sorts of implicit-response-time bias
described above.

In this study the researchers concentrated on the activity of
the amygdala, a subcortical structure and one of the oldest parts
of the brain whose function is to quickly determine whether a
stimulus is positive or threatening. They showed white
Americans photographs of black and white males and examined blood flow to different parts of the participants' brains.
This analysis showed that when the amygdala was activated
following presentation of black (as opposed to white) faces this
was positively related to response-time bias. In other words,
the more bias demonstrated towards outgroups, the brighter the

amygdala 'lit up'. When an animal's amygdala is damaged it ignores threats and dangers, eats its own faeces and tries to copulate with members of other species. A cockroach touching a bit of food on the dining table is enough to put us off the whole meal, even if it wasn't our food that it had a go at. In 1998 Ito and colleagues found that a negative stimulus such as a dead cat elicited more electrophysiological activity than a positive stimulus such as a cuddly puppy. We can see from this how central is the amygdala to threat detection – that is, learning which things are bad and to be avoided. The association of amygdala activation with implicit racial bias suggests once again that we have evolved to see outgroups as a basic threat, like snakes, spiders and other aversive creatures in the world around us.

Other research suggests that this learning system is designed to be particularly sensitive to outgroups. A recent study found that our brains rapidly learn to associate people from outgroups with fear, and that this association is slow to dissipate – just as it is for other biologically relevant predators like snakes and spiders.[35] In one study a conditioned response to white and black faces was elicited via electric shocks and noise. Participants' skin-conductance recordings showed that the conditioned fear of ingroup faces was readily extinguished; however, the learned fear of outgroup targets took longer to extinguish. The dissipation of fear responses to outgroup faces was significantly slower than that to non-threatening biological agents like birds. In other words, the association between outgroup and fear was stronger and more resistant to modification than it was to other stimuli. This is consistent with the idea that outgroups represent a significant threat and that we therefore need to be particularly sensitive to their presence. Notably, the effect occurred only with male outgroups – consistent with the idea that, for our ancestors, males were most likely to pose a survival threat.

A related set of studies adds further support to this notion that we have an evolved fear of outgroups that stems from a basic survival mechanism. People's fear of contracting disease, it seems, is positively related with response-time associations between foreigners and danger.[36] Specifically, asking people to think about contagious disease and immediately afterwards asking them to evaluate foreign (but not familiar) outgroups led in these studies to the endorsement of policies unfavourable to foreigners – for example, stricter immigration, reduced access to healthcare. Disease avoidance is a key programmed behavioural protection mechanism that we all have. This piece of research suggests that outgroups are viewed as more likely to present a disease threat than members of our ingroup.

The idea that outgroups automatically activate the amygdala, a part of the brain associated with disease and danger, resonates with investigations into infrahumanisation. Earlier I discussed how immigrants are seen as somehow psychologically distinct from ingroup members. Research has shown that when people see other humans, the medial prefrontal cortex (mPFC), lights up, but less so when they see immigrants. Furthermore, only people, not objects, activate the mPFC. This suggests a biological correlation with infrahumanisation: immigrants and other outgroups are not associated with the activation of a specific part of the brain that other groups are. The research described above on the delayed dissipation of the fear response to outgroups supports this: whereas learned fear responses to non-dangerous stimuli such as birds and butterflies are readily extinguished, responses to dangerous animals such as spiders and snakes resist extinction.

The biological learning mechanisms we have just discussed are, from an evolutionary viewpoint, the adaptive responses of a human brain focused on building a predictable model of the world. Such mechanisms ensured the greatest chance of survival in our ancestors' dangerous world. Unfortunately, however, their application today leads to prejudice, exclusion, intolerance and the avoidance of intercultural contact.

THE INEVITABILITY OF PREJUDICE?

The research I have examined so far is evidence of the evolution of a more general adaptive drive to predict and make sense of the world. Not only is the evidence that we avoid outgroups consistent with more general evolutionary theory, it also indicates that many of our fixed biases are implicit and operate outside of our conscious awareness. In studies of infrahumanisation people are typically unaware of their tendency to attribute secondary emotions only to ingroups. In studies of implicit bias, people respond to computerised stimuli within under a second – too fast for them to be able to modify or think about the button they are pressing. The evidence for an evolved perception of outgroupers as a threat, resulting in biases that we are not even aware of, has led some psychologists to speculate on the 'inevitability' of prejudice. How can we challenge or change something that's hardwired into the very fabric of our social brains, that has evolved to protect our ancestors through millennia? Does the evolved nature of dehumanisation and its apparently automatic activation mean there is no hope of reducing prejudice, that we are programmed always to see outgroups as a threat?

Well, there *is* hope. Two observations that I make below demonstrate that people's propensity to see outgroups as a threat is not an inflexible rule; not a behavioural response applying universally and with no regard to our immediate environment – indeed, I argue that such a response would be profoundly *un*adaptive.

First, with respect to the human–animal divide that we looked at earlier: when the *similarity* between animals and humans is emphasised to people, without directly mentioning human outgroups, it heightens the willingness to intervene to help minority or stigmatised groups. Furthermore, under these conditions immigrants come to be seen as significantly 'more human' (through the increased attribution of secondary emotions) – a process that could be described as *re-humanisation*.[37]

Second, with respect to the associative-learning bias mentioned above, other researchers have found that the delayed dissipation of the outgroup fear response occurs much less when participants have experience of *interracial dating*.[38] This suggests that intergroup contact can trigger a switch out of the mindset that predisposes us to fear outgroups. Indeed, there is a great deal of research that suggests outgroup contact is the key to mitigating outgroup threat.

It is the capacity for intergroup contact to challenge our preconceptions, stereotypes and biases – to 'turn off' the propensity to see outgroups as a threat – that I turn to in the next chapter. This recent social-psychological evidence forms the basis for the proposition I'll develop in the rest of the book: that we have evolved not only a propensity to fear outgroups, but another propensity as well. This second propensity is a drive to cooperate and build coalitions; to embrace diversity and eschew homogeneity. It is a drive that, properly harnessed, may hold the key to unlocking untapped human potential.

SUMMARY

In this chapter I've introduced the scientific studies that explain why, when and how people accept or reject diversity as the defining characteristic of modern society. Predicated on a basic human need to make sense of the world, social categories are fundamental to how we think about that world. Studies show that if you strip away the historical, political, economic and cultural factors that constitute how people think about diversity, one thing remains: the tendency to organise into 'us' and 'them'.

To accept diversity would be to accept uncertainty and ambiguity. 'Us versus them' is easy: we are like this, they are like that. The roots of this drive can be traced to an innate characteristic of human cognition, embedded and entrenched through thousands of years of human evolution. We have seen how we automatically and unconsciously classify people into groups. I have traced this propensity back to its roots in pre-history. Research has supported evolutionary psychologists' proposition that one of the most significant threats to safety in evolutionary history came from hostile 'outgroup' members and that this fear remains hardwired in the modern mind. People who are different from us (on any number of criteria) activate the same brain systems as the biological threats that would have been prevalent in prehistory. Other studies show that immigrants fail to activate a part of the brain that usually 'lights up' when we see other humans. This evidence suggests that our propensity to think in terms of 'us and them' is based on brain mechanisms evolved to protect our ancestors in a world where 'others' were as dangerous as predators with talons, teeth and claws.

From this perspective diversity is therefore aversive because it contravenes the core drive towards stability, structure and security that lies at the heart of the human psyche – a drive that is tied to our survival as a species in an ancestral world over-run with aggression. But I have also hinted at the malleability of this threat response and at the growing evidence that challenges existing accounts of human socio-cognitive evolution. It is to this evidence that I'll turn next.

CHAPTER 4

A CHALLENGE TO THE INEVITABILITY
OF PREJUDICE

In Chapter 3 I described how humans' social cognition evolved in ancestral environments to regard outgroups as dangerous entities. This basic principle defines the way humans think about difference. Thus, on a basic psychological level it is crucial to how we think about diversity, about people from different groups, backgrounds and cultures. It implies that prejudice, discrimination – everything that follows from this need to create a stable and predictable world – are unchangeable. But if we have evolved to avoid anyone who is not known or similar to us, or a member of the 'ingroup tribe', what hope is there for people of different cultures to live together in harmony?

The research I'll describe in this chapter challenges the basic idea that prejudice is inevitable. It demonstrates that while some people, some of the time, engage outgroup fear and avoidance, others engage an altogether alternative way of thinking. This research is critically important because it provides a direct challenge to existing evolutionary accounts of the hardwired nature of intergroup prejudice. It also provides the basis for building a new evolutionary theory of the emergence of human social cognition, as well as offering a novel perspective on the origins of human civilisation. The research also identifies the socio-ecological 'triggers' for engaging in advanced cognition. In so doing it provides the basis for a new approach to diversity training, multicultural education and government policy – and may help us unlock the potential for innovation and creativity that lies within us all.

ADAPTING TO DIVERSITY

So far we have seen that people have a basic inclination to avoid difference and diversity from the get-go. The human brain, for the most part, doesn't even let us get close to people from different (and potentially dangerous) tribes. In childhood our learning mechanisms quickly establish a negative associ-ation with people from outgroups. Cognitive biases establish a link between people who diverge from the norm and threaten the stability and predictability of our social worlds. Within the first few milliseconds of meeting strangers our brains swing into action to identify their 'tribal status' – and if they're identified as outgroup, then we think in terms of stereotypes and ensure that a safe psychological distance buffers us from harm.

Diversity, in this mindset, doesn't stand a chance. But I'm about to show that under some conditions there's a second way of thinking that attenuates this basic drive to avoid outgroups. Evidence for such a different system can be found in situations where we have no choice but to engage with diversity – in other words, where we have no choice but to think about, and integrate, diversity into our social worlds. This is precisely the case when people leave one culture to go and live in another; that is, when they *migrate*.

Psychologists have been studying the effects of immigration on thinking styles for decades. The research focuses on *acculturation*, the process through which immigrants try to resolve the cognitive conflict between the ideologies that define their original cultural identity and those to which they must adapt in the new culture. There is conflict because often the original culture contains many customs, traditions and ways of thinking that can be directly oppositional to the customs, traditions and norms of the new country.

As a simple example, imagine you are on a business trip to Japan for the first time. On meeting your counterparts you extend your arm to shake hands – an automatic norm in the US or the UK. But in Japan that's not what you do (you bow). Each cultural context comes with different norms and customs that have to be negotiated. We may be able to muddle through when on vacation or taking a business trip, where experiences are culturally simplified and buffered by tourist companies or hosts. But what about when immersion in the host culture is long-term and sustained, like it is when someone immigrates?

The process of psychological change that accompanies migration can result in several distinct outcomes. First of all, one can keep oneself separate from the dominant culture and instead remain within one's community enclave; for instance, a Pakistani immigrant might identify himself only as Pakistani, not British. On the other hand, immigrants can go to the opposite extreme, assimilating entirely to the host culture and thinking of themselves as exclusively British. Assimilation involves adopting the norms, values and practices of the host culture, transitioning one's sense of self and identity. And there's a third strategy: *integration*. Integration involves immigrants adopting the value system of the host culture while simultaneously maintaining their own customs and traditions, in which case the Pakistani immigrant sees himself as both Pakistani *and* British.

These different kinds of social and cultural integration have generated, and continue to generate, a great deal of debate in modern politics. Should immigrants be required to relinquish their former identities, embracing and adopting the host country's values to the fullest extent? Or should they be free to live in accordance with their original cultural values and norms? Alternatively, should some integration of the two be the preferred strategy, so as to facilitate a harmonious society? These are important questions, because they have unique consequences for how people think about intergroup relations.

THE CONTACT HYPOTHESIS

What psychological processes kick in when we meet someone who's different from us – in evolutionary parlance, from a different 'tribe'? This has been the focus of over fifty years of research in social psychology. It all started with the *contact hypothesis*.

In 1954 the social psychologist Gordon Allport published a book about prejudice.[39] It was one of the first psychological accounts of this social issue, and the new hypothesis that he proposed was to become one of the most influential in the discipline. The idea was simple: prejudice, thought Allport, was caused by ignorance. Therefore, getting groups together under the right conditions must be the way forward. He argued that bringing together members of groups differing by race, religion or national origin could serve to reduce negative stereotyping. But of course, it wasn't going to be that simple, given that mere contact was self-evidently the basis for prejudice in the first place (after all, if people never came into contact with one another there would be no conflict). Crucially, Allport argued, contact had to take place under very specific conditions if it was to achieve acceptance and if diversity was to be tolerated.

First, he proposed, social norms favouring equality must be put in place: social and institutional support was a prerequisite. In other words, the social conditions – government policy, schools and laws – should all promote integration. Second, there must be sustained close contact between the different groups, and that contact must be of sufficient frequency, duration and closeness to allow meaningful intergroup relations to develop ('acquaintance potential', as it was termed). Third, contact must occur under conditions of equal social status. If the minority group had contact with the majority group as a subordinate, this would be likely to perpetuate negative stereotypes of inferiority. Fourth, contact must take the form of cooperative interaction.

More than half a century after its publication, *The Nature of Prejudice* has become the most widely cited work on the subject, and it remains a key guide for modern scholars. A recent review of over five hundred studies has confirmed, using sophisticated statistical techniques, that Allport's core proposition is correct: there is a robust relationship between contact and tolerance.

Contact does many positive things for intergroup relations. For a start, it changes attitudes and promotes self-disclosure, trust and empathy. Most importantly, it breaks down the cognitive barriers that are thrown up by the human brain. It makes people see similarities where before they saw only difference. It establishes outgroups as not too different after all, and creates the conditions to integrate them with the ingroup and restore cognitive balance. This cognitive impact of contact has direct implications for the supposition that humans can override evolved tendencies to automatically avoid and fear outgroups.

Earlier I discussed how immigrants moving to a new culture can adopt different strategies to deal with the incompatibility of their existing beliefs and ways of life with those of the host culture. These strategies can be thought of as the mind kicking in where it cannot initiate action to avoid outgroups and difference. Here, the mind has to come up with strategies for dealing with diversity, and one of those strategies is *assimilation*.

Assimilation involves changing one's cognitive representation, one's view of oneself, as 'different' and as a minority, and mentally merging with the new culture, the majority. As our cities, schools and workplaces become more diverse, there is a growing need to construct mental models to help us simplify, structure and make sense of our social environments. Think back to the profound human need to categorise and classify that I discussed in Chapter 3. Merging our mental picture of 'us' and 'them' is an efficient way of dealing with this increased complexity in our environments, and this is precisely what intergroup contact achieves.

For instance, in one experiment[40] participants were randomly allocated to two ad hoc groups ('A' or 'B'), then took part in a problem-solving exercise. Some of them sat around a table in a separated pattern – three A-group members opposite three Bs (AAABBB). Others sat around a table in an integrated pattern (ABABAB). They were required either to work within their original A or B group and give a group solution to the problem; or the two groups were required to work together (in the integrated pattern) and give a single response agreed by both groups. In this way, the experiment modelled the conditions that represent diversity in the real world, and showed what would happen if we asked people to engage in cooperative intergroup contact – that is, forget their original cultural identities and work together.

The researchers found that when they asked the participants what they thought of the other people taking part, those in the separated state (representing the separation of cultural ideologies in society) reported preferences that followed the diversity 'fault line' – that is, they liked people in their own group more than those in the other. In contrast, this fault line melted away in the assimilated state – whether people were identified as belonging to group A or group B bore no relation to how much they were liked. This study shows, albeit in a highly controlled experimental setting, that one way we have of dealing with diversity is to simply reclassify ourselves from 'outsider' to member of a 'common ingroup'. Subsequent research has confirmed the basic positive impact of this assimilation strategy in a range of settings and with a range of groups.

While effective in some settings, there are two significant limitations to this assimilation model. First, it doesn't show us anything different from the established evolutionary theory described earlier. In effect, assimilation adopts precisely the same mindset as the human brain starts with. In other words, following assimilation, the brain simply reclassifies former minorities as members of the common ingroup, so they are no longer a threat. There is no change in the basic tendency to avoid outgroupers, and a general fear of difference and diversity remains.

The second, practical, limitation to the assimilation strategy is this. While cooperation and contact that encourage people to assimilate constitute an effective strategy in the behavioural-science laboratory, the strategy has been criticised for not reflecting how people think about difference in the real world. Quite simply, people have drives and motivations that prevent them from just flipping a switch and reclassifying outgroupers as potential ingroupers. From an evolutionary point of view, if it had been that easy it wouldn't have been an effective protection strategy. While seemingly a simple mental operation – 'I am now British' – the process of transitioning one's mental representation of oneself from separate entity to merged with people in a new culture is considerable. People's drives and desires kick in here and, as we can see, issues such as immigration can arouse intense feelings.

A LOSS OF IDENTITY

So is it realistic to merely get people 'to get along' in modern society. Given the tensions that arise around immigration issues, could this sort of reclassification really overcome powerful ethnic and racial categorisations? For instance, Catholics and Protestants in Northern Ireland might be reluctant to downplay their denominational membership and adopt the identity 'Northern Irish', which includes members of outgroups. When people care deeply about their original identities – whether that be to do with national pride, religion, gender or race – they can be reluctant to adopt overarching identities that include outgroups. Studies using 'artificial' groups (as in the last experiment I described) demonstrate this reaction in people who are what psychologists call 'high identifiers'.

Using a design that mirrored the real-life context of corporate mergers, Dutch researchers have found that pre-merger identification predicted post-merger intergroup attitudes: the higher the level of identification with the original companies, the higher the subsequent (post-merger) antagonism between the former separate companies.[41] Related to this finding, in research that I carried out with my PhD students I compared what would happen when British students read a story about how Britain was edging closer to federalism and a 'United States of Europe'.[42] People who regarded being British as of central importance to their sense of self reacted strongly against the suggestion that they should be merged into a superordinate identity. This even occurred at a subconscious level. In one computerised task, the reaction times of the higher identifying students – those who identified more strongly with 'Britishness' – were faster to British-positive and French-negative associations than to British-negative and French-positive associations.

The reason for such a reaction goes back once again to the human brain's need for certainty and structure. Social categorisation provides a means of reducing uncertainty. Indeed, as we've seen, studies have shown that social categorisation is accentuated in conditions that promote uncertainty. Other studies have shown that people tend to reject multiculturalism to a greater extent when they identify highly with their own group. And remember the North American participants mentioned earlier who identified strongly as being white North Americans, and who, compared to a control group, reacted negatively to thinking about multiculturalism. The idea here is that the more people are invested in their own group – the more important it is to their sense of self – then the more they are liable to see the assimilation of other cultures as a threat. The problem seems to be the implied loss of importance of one's own cultural identity when the outgroup is brought into the ingroup fold.

MANAGING DIVERSITY

If people react against assimilation, the solution may be an alternative cultural adaptation strategy: *integration*. Integration involves cognitively representing people from different groups not as a merged common ingroup, but as a group of distinct, yet connected, social elements. For instance, someone can be black and British, white and British, black and French, white and French. In reality, in a diverse society we cannot simply ignore difference.

This is because we are not just disinterestedly members of different social groups. Rather, we are psychologically invested in our cultural identities, and how we feel about ourselves is intricately and intimately bound up with these identities. Of course, this all makes evolutionary sense. Social categorisation clarifies our social worlds, providing a means for predicting how outgroupers will behave as well as a set of prescriptive ingroup norms to guide our own behaviour. This leads to a strong motivation to differentiate 'us' from 'them' that I described in the previous chapter. It reduces uncertainty and provides predictability.

A good example of this is how the British feel about the European Union, an issue that has given rise to ongoing public and political debate. In my own research, discussed above, I've asked people to read a paragraph advocating closer European integration and the dissolution of member states into a 'United States of Europe' – thereby making the assimilation real, and threatening the distinctiveness of being exclusively British. The result was that the more people identified with being British, the more strongly they rejected the article they'd just read. We discovered, too, that this was the case on a sub-conscious level (using as a measure the Implicit Association Test (IAT) technique discussed in Chapter 3).

There is a way to get around this strong motivation to resist assimilation. If the problem is the dissolution of existing cultural identities, then if we assimilate but at the same time maintain these identities – that is, integrate – this should encourage us to accept close ties. And this is precisely what the research shows: people are happy to be European if they can at the same time maintain their British identity. However, as soon as the sovereignty of the original identity is eroded, this sparks strong rejection of the superordinate category and a desire to break away.

The fact that people can maintain two initially incongruous cultural identities at the same time is a critical insight, because it suggests they can do more than simply ignore differences in their efforts to get along: it suggests, too, that they can rise to the challenge of integration and mentally representing diversity. The way in which we do this, however, requires an entirely different way of thinking.

CHALLENGING DIVERSITY

As we saw in Chapter 2, given the complexity of the social world and our limited cognitive resources, people categorise when thinking about others. Categorical thinking enables impressions to be construed on the basis of labels like sex, race or occupation, rather than forming individuated impressions. This is how the human brain works, by default, automatically springing to life to categorise and classify when we meet someone.

However, when people are classified according to two dimensions of categorisation – which is required by the integration strategy outlined above – something else has to happen. Imagine, for instance, that you come across a male midwife. He would immediately grab your attention and engage a mode of thinking entirely different from the default system. Now, the aim is to figure out who this person is; in evolutionary terms, your mind is working out how to classify him. The aims of the default system are consistent with the overarching function of the human brain: to create a model of the world that is as predictable as possible. So when someone does not fit into the existing mental model, different processes need to be engaged to work out why and to revise that model accordingly.

Studies tell us that when we are encouraged to ignore this tendency to categorise and get to know someone who doesn't fit in with our mental model of the world, such as a woman mechanic or a gay soldier, this makes us cognitively shift gear and show less reliance on stereotypes.[43] These kinds of conflicting categorisations lead to the generation of *emergent attributes*, which are attributes ascribed to surprising category combinations. These are independent of the stereotypes that comprise either of the components of the surprising combination. In the classic example, a 'Harvard-educated carpenter' may be perceived as non-materialistic, but this is not something that springs to mind when someone is described as simply 'Harvard-educated' or simply 'a carpenter'. It is an *emergent* property of the surprising category combination, and shows the human mind revising its mental model of the world. By creating an entirely new category the stability of the mental system, and predictability, are restored.

In the context of acculturation, whether we are talking about a white British-majority-group member forming an impression of a British Muslim, or a British Muslim making sense of his or her place as a Muslim in Britain, both individuals will need to go through the same cognitive process. They will both have to reconcile conflicting stereotypic assumptions associated with being British and being Muslim, and they will do this via the process of inhibiting the relevant stereotype and generating the emergent attribute.

This work offers a potentially useful tool for encouraging tolerance, and there is research evidence to support the idea that the model could be usefully applied to education. For instance, primary school children can be taught to classify along many dimensions using pictures of men and women engaging in typically and traditionally feminine jobs such as hairstylist or secretary, and typically masculine jobs such as construction worker or truck driver. After this 'counter-stereotype' training they were found to be less likely to stereotype women and men on the basis of occupation.[44]

The research I've described above suggests that we have not evolved a single, hardwired system for dealing with people from different groups and cultures. Rather, under the right circumstances – namely, where the social context involves diversity that challenges expectations and stereotypes – a second system may come into play that aims to resolve the inconsistencies we meet with when our impressions of a person are being formed. When no category can be fitted to that person because he or she is showing characteristics or behaviour that is counter-stereotypical to his or her apparent category membership (e.g., she's a truck driver, or simply someone from a feared or disliked group who is acting friendly), then our brains must abandon stereotypes. If need be, our brains must then create a new category so that similar individuals encountered in the future can be categorised and predictability can be maintained.

SUMMARY

In this chapter I've talked about a range of research findings from contemporary social psychology that challenges the view that humans are programmed to dislike, distrust and be aggressive towards outgroups. This research suggests that under the right conditions people revise how they think about people from other cultures and form a common ingroup identity that includes former outgroupers. This assimilation effectively redirects the processes that normally lead people to favour their own group, resulting in greater tolerance in intercultural relations. However, while the evidence inspires hope that this cognitive shift in perspective may lead to more positive relations, arguably the process does not solve the underlying problems of prejudice and intolerance. Rather, it may simply redirect those problems to another level – for example, to religion rather than nationality as a basis for bias. It's just moving the goalposts, you might say.

More recent work, however, has raised the possibility that a different brain system can be used when people think about intercultural relations. The suggestion is that when we are surprised by someone we shift mental gear, out of our threat-focused way of thinking, in order to adopt a more creative, open-minded approach. In other words, we can draw on an entirely different cognitive system, one that focuses not on fear and avoidance but on exploration and change. Critically, this research shows that under the right conditions stereotypes can be challenged, and dismissed; it suggests that there is not just one evolved system for dealing with group differences.

In the next few chapters I'm going to argue that, while the human brain has a default way of thinking about groups that relies on social stereotypes, a second system, adapted to promote tolerance and cooperation, also exists. Furthermore, this second brain system is far more central to how our minds evolved than previously thought.

CHAPTER 5

THE GREAT LEAP FORWARD

What made the modern mind? We know that our bodies evolved, adapting to the environment to best ensure survival, but what about our minds? Evolutionary psychologists study how our behaviour and thinking systems have evolved to accommodate the characteristics and challenges of the world around us. In this chapter I introduce these ideas, and the anthropological studies that make a compelling case that our advanced cognitive abilities emerged through the course of human *social* evolution.

THE SOCIAL ANIMAL

Evolutionary psychology argues that our brains and behaviour are shaped by the environmental challenges that faced our ancestors. An important realisation here was that for a social species like humans, being adaptive to the environment can be defined at the group level. In other words, people may evolve in ways that equip them poorly to survive as an individual, but possess behavioural traits that make them highly adaptive as part of a collective.

To illustrate this, take human learning. Clearly, young children cannot survive without their parents until they reach a certain point in their development. This applies not only to their physical development but also to their cognitive development. In fact, there is emerging evidence that certain aspects of children's cognitive development may have specifically evolved to be *late*-developing. There is no benefit to the individual in this late cognitive development – after all, the quicker one gets smarter, the better for survival. However, the late development of some cognitive abilities can enhance the survival needs of the *group*.

An ingenious developmental psychology study demonstrates the point. This study looked at how children learn to use tools to solve problems.[45] In particular, the researchers aimed to see whether children could innovate to make a new tool for extracting a small bucket on a loop from within a tube, without having seen the solution performed by someone else (the solution involves bending a piece of wire into a hook shape). The study found that children below five years old were unable to solve the problem. By eight, however, most of them were able to work it out. Importantly, when five-year-olds were shown by adults how to solve the task, they were able to copy them and create the wire hook. In other words, children's ability to *innovate* developed much later than their ability to *learn*.

Children's creative ability in this sort of task draws upon advanced mental abilities. They must see the problem from many angles and develop a new way of viewing the piece of wire – not simply as a piece of wire, with all the characteristics of wire that reside in their memories, but as an object that can be transformed into something entirely new.

So why do our learning and innovation systems develop at different rates? One might think this is profoundly maladaptive and conveys no evolutionary advantage at all. Being unable to innovate, as an individual, is quite a disadvantage from a survival perspective. However, the late development of creative cognition makes perfect sense when we consider evolutionary fitness at the group level.

Think about the history of human civilisation. We stand upon the shoulders of giants: we are able to sustain the planet's population only because of the technological advances made by earlier generations. A species that is designed to live together, to forge social relationships for mutual benefit and protection, will prosper and grow if it can learn from the generation before and build on that knowledge. Innovations create progress, and then accumulated knowledge can be passed on to the next generation, and so on.

How does the individual benefit from the accumulated achievements of earlier generations? The answer is: via the delaying of the development of creative cognition. It would be profoundly inefficient for each individual in the collective to reinvent the wheel. So much so that it's much better if they don't even try. For the group, all that effort involved in figuring out solutions to problems that have already been solved is a total waste. More importantly, it is time that could more productively be spent learning the solutions to problems that have already been solved by earlier generations. This time is crucial for two reasons. First, it provides the time 'credit' needed to innovate and solve problems that have not yet been solved by the collective. Second, it provides the knowledge needed on which to base these solutions (all innovation requires a knowledge base from which to start).

This argument demonstrates a critical point: that the evolution of cognitive systems can be driven entirely by the survival needs of the collective rather than of the individual. It tells us that the collective is critical to understanding human cognitive development, and that evolutionary pathways can be selected at the level of the group, society or civilisation over the individual. It tells us how societal needs influenced the evolution of individual developmental stages. However, it does not tell us *why* these advanced cognitive abilities developed in the first place. A basic learning ability exists in dogs and cats, but only humans have such an advanced capacity to think creatively. The question regarding our human ancestors is: what precipitated the development of creative cognition? The answer may be that, just as the needs of the collective define the development of creative cognition in children, so too do they explain the emergence of this system in our evolution as a species. This idea is referred to as the Social Brain Hypothesis.

THE SOCIAL BRAIN HYPOTHESIS

Humans have extremely large brains relative to the size of their bodies. In fact, they are considerably larger than what is needed to simply stay alive. Of course, advanced cognitive abilities require more brain real estate, and that's precisely why our brains are so big. But they did not grow big for no reason – they grew because in the course of our evolution creative cognition came to confer a functional advantage for survival.

Traditional anthropology suggests that our ancestors' large brains evolved because of the functional advantages of being able to create tools, invent ways to trap food and predict climatic variation – all the things that would have enhanced the capacity to survive, procreate, and become the dominant species on the planet. The problem is that this account doesn't provide a compelling reason why, in evolutionary terms, this capability developed in the first place. Yes, it confers a survival advantage, but it took thousands of years for humans to evolve the system in what was essentially an unchanging physical habitat. Something must have changed in this environment to suddenly make creative cognition necessary for survival, rather than humans relying on the more basic learning abilities shared with animals that had served them quite well for some time.

According to the Social Brain Hypothesis, what changed was the nature of human society, precipitated by population growth. At some point in our evolutionary history we reached a population-growth tipping point. At this juncture humans who were able to form effective collectives would stand a much greater chance of survival than those who decided to go it alone.

OK, so population growth expands to such a point that the opportunity arises to create tribes rather than loose family collectives – but why should this require advanced creative cognition?

The answer is social interaction.

As I mentioned earlier, humans have become the dominant species on the planet because they are able to transmit knowledge over successive generations; to learn from that knowledge, and then build on it for future generations. We are an inherently social species, and social relationships are essential to our survival and progress. According to recent anthropological studies, it is precisely the need to develop, cement and exploit social relationships that required the brain's adaptation to creative cognition. In other words, we developed advanced forms of thinking because it enabled our ancestors to build bonds and form collectives.[46]

The Social Brain Hypothesis[47] proposes that key elements of human cognition (and to a lesser extent the cognition of other primates[48]) evolved to enable us to adapt to the demands of living in groups. According to R. I. M. Dunbar (1998), instead of each individual human having to solve survival conundrums on his or her own, our ancestors found that it was far more efficient to solve such problems *socially*. So creative cognition emerged to enable them to build social bonds that enhanced adaptive fitness. This sort of coordinated group life requires cooperation and planning – abilities that are the hallmark of advanced cognitive capabilities. Unlike the individual human, groups must look beyond self-interest, take the long view and envisage new identities, aims and goals. Coordination, negotiation and planning require the ability to inhibit one's existing ideas: one's own perspective must be set aside and the needs of one's potential partner must be considered. To build bonds we must anticipate that things will be different from how they are now, so as to generate alternative realities and prospects for the future, such as working together and envisaging what a partnership could look like. These are the critical elements of the cognitive abilities that our ancestors needed to build tribal coalitions – and they are precisely the processes identified by modern cognitive science as crucial to creativity.

In primates the hypothesis is supported by evidence that brain mass correlates with the complexity of social behaviour. But how does managing social relations within large groups map onto the evolution of specific types of advanced cognitive ability?

Well, according to the hypothesis, as population numbers increased and humans began to band together in larger collectives, the need to maintain cohesion became an increasingly difficult challenge. The conventional non-human primate mechanism for establishing and servicing friendships and coalitions is social grooming. As humans created groups made up of larger and more complex networks, this grooming, which takes time and requires a one-to-one relationship, became increasingly inefficient. It was the need for a mechanism to maintain order that precipitated the evolution of language. Language facilitates bonding in large groups because it allows individuals to 'groom' multiple group members simultaneously, and allows the exchange of information without the need for physical contact. This, in turn, allows groups to maintain a larger social network.

Anthropological evidence is continuing to amass in support of the notion that it was our social ecology, not our natural one, that created the conditions for advanced cognition to evolve. For instance, when the same battery of cognitive tests is given to a three-year-old and a chimpanzee, the results are precisely what the Social Brain Hypothesis would predict. Both humans and chimpanzees perform about the same in tests of physical cognition involving space and quantities, but the children display greater sophistication when dealing with the social world, even before they have started to learn more complex forms of written language and mathematics in formal education.

This all makes sense. The evolutionary challenge for humans was not just climate, food shortages, parasites or predators, but also the need to negotiate complex interpersonal communication and intra-group dynamics. While all species must compete for resources in order to survive and reproduce, humans must foster social relations above all else to ensure survival.

Supporting this idea, that social bonds were critical to human evolution, is research on the effects of ostracism, in the sense of being excluded from social groups. Social acceptance and the need to belong are adaptive mechanisms, fundamental for survival and reproduction throughout human evolution. When an individual is excluded or ostracised, the need to belong is threatened, an experience that can have detrimental consequences for that individual. Ostracism therefore threatens people's fundamental needs, including self-esteem, control and the need for a meaningful existence. The impact of ostracism is almost visceral – it can cause people to feel social pain on a par with physical pain. It's an evolved system designed to ensure safety in numbers.

In contrast, the power of the ingroup tribe not only to provide security but even to repair physical harm is striking. For example, cancer patients join relevant support groups to increase their knowledge of their predicament but also to gain a sense of community and belonging. There is much evidence that socially supportive relationships can reduce stress levels and protect physical and mental health, either directly or by buffering the effects of stress on well-being. Overall, social support can satisfy emotional and cognitive needs, and it has been associated with recovery from illness. In sum, the ability to create and maintain social bonds is, and remains, hardwired into the human brain.

So that's the Social Brain Hypothesis – the idea that advances in human cognition evolved primarily as a way of helping humans create social bonds. This is because social cognition is defined by the ability to maintain, manage and cultivate cohesion within groups. Social bonds lie at the heart of how we came to be the pre-eminent species on the planet.

I'm now going to extend this argument with one simple step, but it's a step that has profound implications. I will argue that we humans are perfectly adapted to build civilisations through our capacity to work together and coordinate cohesive groups – but I'm going to go further than this. I'm going to argue that it was not just any social interaction that proved central to our cognitive evolution, but specifically interactions with *out-groups*. I'm going to argue, in an extension to existing accounts of the origins of conflict, that it was the need to *cooperate* with outgroup tribes that enabled advanced cognition to evolve, and that it is this that can explain one of the mysteries of modern anthropology.

THE GREAT LEAP FORWARD

Many anthropologists have come to believe that modern humans are descended from a single species of Homo sapiens who migrated out of the African continent between 50,000 and 100,000 years ago.[49] These Homo sapiens came to replace the world's two competing human species: Homo erectus in Asia and the Neanderthals in Europe. Support for this *Out of Africa* hypothesis comes from the finding that all modern humans' genealogies can be traced back to a single female African progenitor (a mitochondrial Eve). The theory is that a massive eruption took place where Lake Toba now is, in Indonesia, about seventy thousand years ago. This eruption killed most humans on the planet, leaving just a small band from whom all modern humans' mitochondrial DNA derives.

This is important because it suggests that at a specific point in history there were so few humans on the planet that they would all have been faced with precisely the same environmental challenges. Estimates are that the remaining human population was down to 2000–5000 at this time. As such we can theorise with greater certainty about the environmental conditions that would have influenced the evolution of human cognition. One particular event is widely regarded by anthropologists as pivotal to the emergence of the behavioural and cognitive systems that define modern humans, and in turn the development of human civilisation as we know it: this event is known as the Great Leap Forward.

The Great Leap Forward describes the sudden surge in human intelligence observed in the anthropological record about a hundred thousand years ago.[50] The record shows a significant advance in areas like agricultural technology, along with the emergence of the sophisticated social systems that laid the basis for modern civilisation; rudimentary theology, philosophy and laws, for instance. Rituals such as burials involving grave gifts, the belief in an afterlife and the realisation of mortality are all indicated as well. The use of pigment for self-decoration, jewellery, cave paintings and figurines begin to be seen about this time. Hunting-related technologies advance significantly – for example, the use of fishhooks; and similarly we start to see the development of trade systems such as bartering and the emergence of long-distance trading networks. Evidence of cooking and the use of seasonings is seen, as well as the use of animal hides to make clothing, bone buttons and needles.

All of the developments and findings I've just described required the use of abstraction, symbolic thought, innovation and creativity, and all of them point to a great leap forward in cognitive ability. It was this great leap of human intelligence.

What is intriguing is that before the Big Bang, Homo sapiens were behaviourally primitive, indistinguishable from the Neanderthals or Homo erectus in the sophistication of their cognitive abilities. They lacked the mental skills to produce advanced artwork and the tools characteristically used by later humans. There was no evidence of theological thinking or of the structuring and management of social coalitions, collectives and networks. Before the Great Leap Forward, humans essentially lived in evolutionary stasis for millennia. What was it, then, that led to this significant acceleration in cognitive evolution?

This is a question that scholars from many disciplines have grappled with for years. Here I'm going to propose a new *psychological* explanation, one based upon the principles and processes that we've explored in this book so far, one based on intercultural contact.

THE EVOLUTIONARY CONTACT HYPOTHESIS

Genetic and fossil evidence shows Homo sapiens to have evolved into anatomically modern humans only in Africa, about 200,000 to 150,000 years ago. One branch then left Africa sometime between 100,000 and 50,000 years ago and became the dominant species of human, winning the survival race over the competing species of Neanderthals and Homo erectus.

It is the co-occurrence of this migration out of Africa and the great leap in human cognitive abilities that has led many anthropologists to believe that the two events are linked. It is thought that the Great Leap Forward was triggered by environmental conditions in Africa such as increasing aridity, which meant new techniques were needed to ensure survival. In evolutionary terms, it was those humans who developed the capacity to solve these problems that were most likely to survive. We adapted as a species to the physical environment – so goes the traditional view of human evolution. However, evidence of environmental change around this time remains sparse, and so this explanation remains speculative. The one thing we do know for sure is that it was about now that the human population began to grow at an exponential rate. It is this population explosion that, I argue, holds the key to the mystery of the Great Leap Forward.

As noted in the previous chapter, it is not just changes in our ancestors' physical environment that can explain cognitive evolution, it is also changes to their *social* environment. The Social Brain Hypothesis maintains that as populations grew and humans increasingly found there were benefits to living together in collectives (economies of scale, advantages of specialisation, strength in numbers) more brainpower was required to hold these collectives together. Of course, humans didn't simply mass together in one great collective; what emerged were growing micro-societies, many tribes that governed by their own separate norms, rules and ideologies.

What the Social Brain Hypothesis doesn't deal with is how humans' cognitive systems adapted to deal with *intercultural* activity. In other words, what happened when different tribes began to come into contact with one another? Present evolutionary psychology holds that this was the catalyst that brought about the enduring human propensity to fear and avoid outgroups, and to aggress towards them. As we saw in

Chapter 3, according to this account modern intergroup conflict is all down to our evolved (and adaptive) fear of difference and diversity. As populations grew, groups would have increasingly found themselves competing for scarce natural resources in the shape of food, fuel and shelter. This would inevitably have led to conflict. Thus our ancestors evolved to be highly attuned to outgroup threats. Recall the pervasiveness of the social categorisation processes outlined in Chapter 3. Simplifying the world into categories provides an evolutionary advantage. It enables prediction, and prediction aids survival; it enabled our ancestors to rapidly distinguish friend from foe, and in so doing helped them to activate an appropriate fight-or-flight response. This overwhelming tendency to see the world as us and them is a specific adaption of the more general need for homogeneity, stability, simplicity and structure.

As I suggested in Chapter 4, though, modern social psychology has found that this singular threat response is not the only way to think about outgroups. Under some conditions intercultural behaviour is not defined by threat, but rather framed by openness and inclusiveness. We possess not only the conservative, protect-and-defend response to difference; our social brains can also respond with empathy, perspective-taking and an ability to envisage positive relations. We can hold back fears that derive from the past and project a different, positive future. This apparent ability to suspend an automatic fear of difference and instead to engage in positive intercultural contact suggests that our ancestors could have evolved a separate and distinct 'coalition-building' system designed to build intercultural bridges, when it was more adaptive to do so rather than fight or fly. We can call this the Evolutionary Contact Hypothesis.

In fact, the existence of this second system makes a lot of sense. If we had evolved just one way of dealing with difference, where would we be today? If all groups in contact with each other ever did was compete, this would lead gradually but inevitably to mutual destruction. As Stephen Pinker has argued in *The Better Angels of Our Nature*:[51] yes, human conflict exists around the world and is sometimes shocking in its brutality. Yes, it seems to be getting even more prevalent, in an age where the Internet reveals more of our world than ever before. But the occurrence of conflict is actually slowing down. Our ancestors may also have had an evolved cognitive system for avoiding outgroup threats, and this may well persist to this day because it conferred on them an evolutionary advantage. However, we humans may well also have evolved a second system that enabled adaptation to intercultural contact in an altogether different way: not always to compete, but seeing a different way to coexist. What Pinker's analysis suggests is that on the whole this second system may even be winning the fight for human nature.

In sum, it would simply not be adaptive *always* to see outgroups as enemies. There will have been situations in which only by working together could different tribes solve the survival problems they faced: for instance, pooling resources in times of famine. It would therefore have been highly adaptive for human tribes to possess the mental abilities to bring about reconciliation and peaceful coexistence – like perspective-taking and the skills to negotiate fair and equitable division of resources.

These abilities are precisely those considered to have evolved, through social interaction, by the Social Brain Hypothesis. The process of building one-to-one relationships is the same whether one is in a group of two, ten or ten thousand. But such abilities would have been *even more* necessary in forging intercultural coalitions, because in intercultural activities of any kind one has to overcome a competing process – the brain's automatic tendency to characterise outgroups as a threat. Overcoming the power of social categorisation requires qualitatively the same processes as are involved in building interpersonal bonds, but of a much greater magnitude. From this perspective the Great Leap Forward is simply the by-product of a rapid advance in cognition needed to negotiate intercultural interaction – it is a matter of scale, not process. Of course these abilities existed before the Great Leap; it's just that the pace of development was constrained by the lack of intercultural contact. With population growth and increased group-based interaction, a great leap forward was required in the intellectual abilities used to build those intercultural bonds.

SUMMARY

Evolutionary social psychology argues that many of the behavioural tendencies we observe in modern humans are a response to the environmental adaptations that faced our ancestors. The argument is that humans have evolved so rapidly over the last fifty thousand years that our cognitive systems and behavioural tendencies are catching up with modern society and civilisation. Social cognition and behaviour (such as prejudice, conflict, leadership, cooperation) are adaptations of the social relations that our ancestors had to form in order to survive. I've argued that for them it would not have been adaptive to always see outgroups as the opposition; sometimes it would have been beneficial to forge allegiances across group boundaries – for instance, to unite against a common enemy or increase the skills base of a nominal common ingroup. Therefore, alongside a threat-detection system humans should possess a second, coalition-building, system, one that can override outgroup fear when it is adaptive to do so (e.g., to facilitate, enhance and extend the group's productivity, skills and security).

Furthermore, the evolutionary logic of this dual-system response to intercultural contact offers us an insight into one of the mysteries of modern anthropology. A hundred thousand years ago we emerged from millennia as hunter-gatherers to embark on the most significant cultural, technological and intellectual evolutionary period in human prehistory. This pivotal event has been characterised as the Great Leap Forward. At this point the archaeological record shows a significant advance in technological innovation: fine tool making, sophisticated weaponry, sculpture, cave painting, long-distance trade, and hunting with more refined techniques. It was the beginning of behavioural modernity, the beginning of the modern human mind.

But what caused this sudden advance? I argue that it's because of the evolution of brain systems required to deal effectively with intercultural contact. The coalition-building system enabled our ancestors to form social bonds that enhanced the survival prospects of the group, to look beyond self-interest and envisage new collective identities, goals and purposes. In so doing they developed precisely those mental abilities that are critical to success in the modern world – our potential to innovate, create, develop and grow.

If the dynamics required to form intercultural coalitions advanced cognition in humans, can we find any evidence in contemporary behaviour for this link? Any theory must be testable, and it should be possible to observe in today's inter-cultural world the coalitional system specified by this evolutionary account. Evaluating the evidence for this system is the focus of Chapter 6.

CHAPTER 6

CULTIVATING CREATIVITY

In Chapter 5 I argued that The Great Leap Forward was predicated on an increase in inter-tribal contact resulting from a rapid rise in the human population about a hundred thousand years ago. Ever-expanding inter-tribal contact meant that groups had to do one of two things: compete, or cooperate. While most research to date has assumed the primacy of conflict in shaping human cognition, I've argued that cooperation may have been equally, or even more, important. Specifically, I've suggested that our ancestors adapted to diversity through the emergence of a second cognitive system, one designed to help forge coalitions, not engage in conflict. The Evolutionary Contact Hypothesis proposes that humans evolved cognitive capabilities to overcome a more primitive system of threat detection and avoidance, to build intergroup bridges and forge coalitional groups characterised by diversity. Building inter-group bridges requires people to overcome an automatic system designed to detect friend from foe and to protect us from out-group aggressors. The mental effort and abilities required to suppress this detect-and-protect system are considerable, which explains the rapid acceleration of cognitive abilities characterised by the Great Leap Forward.

The emergence of the coalition-building system provides the pivotal point that enabled us to achieve advances in technology, agriculture and engineering. This great leap in human intelligence is integrally linked to our social evolution. I've argued that humans evolved their modern intellect precisely when they learned to overcome their innate fear of outgroups, to cooperate with others, to see beyond boundaries.

I've argued, too, that our brains are built upon our ancestors' experience of forging social relations across the us–them divide; that they are, intrinsically, social brains. Now I'm going to look at the evidence supporting this Evolutionary Contact Hypothesis, evidence provided by modern behavioural science. If it's true that adapting to diversity was pivotal to the evolution of our advanced cognitive abilities, then we should be able to identify relevant 'ecological triggers' in modern humans. In other words, under the right conditions – conditions that mirror those that led to the selection of advanced cognition for our ancestors – we should be able to observe evidence of enhanced cognitive performance (i.e. creativity, problem-solving and so forth) in people today.

WHAT STIMULATES COALITIONAL THINKING?

So the argument is that our ancestors would often have needed to engage coalitional thinking when their tribe came into contact with other tribes. Of course, their behaviour may often have relied entirely on the threat-detection system, and this is when conflict would have ensued. However, as I discussed in Chapter 4, conflict is sometimes patently counterproductive, and under some conditions forging workable relations between groups is both adaptive and mutually beneficial. The modern manifestation of this mindset is multiculturalism.

The idea that multiculturalism can foster harmonious relations isn't new; and although the argument has never been rooted in evolutionary terms, social scientists from a range of disciplines have postulated its value for society. Amartya Sen, the Nobel Prize-winning economist, is widely cited as a proponent of the view that diversity promotes social harmony. Sociologists and social psychologists agree. The multiculturalism hypothesis asserts that a society defined by distinct cultural, ethnic and religious identities promotes tolerance. However, it is also true that social sciences research has supported the classic evolutionary view of the inevitability of conflict between groups, where diversity has been found to endanger social cohesion and promote poor intergroup relations.

The research I've talked about here shows that intercultural contact can – but need not – lead to conflict. In what follows I suggest that experiencing diversity in a way that triggers the coalitional brain system encourages people to be not only more tolerant, but also more flexible and creative. Specifically, when intercultural contact *requires* people to look beyond existing stereotypes, and providing they are motivated and able to do so, the coalitional system will be activated, along with all the advanced cognitive capabilities that I've discussed so far.

BICULTURALS AND COGNITIVE FLEXIBILITY

To understand how diversity stimulates the activation of the coalitional system we look again to contemporary psychological science. Let's start by considering how inter-cultural contact changes how people think. In Chapter 4 I introduced the concept of *acculturation*, the process whereby immigrants resolve the cognitive conflict between the norms and ideologies that define their original cultural identity and those to which they must adapt in the new culture. This process of psychological change can result in four possible outcomes. To recap, immigrants can *assimilate* into the host culture (think of the Pakistani British man who identifies himself only as British). I suggested that this was simply redirecting the pro-cesses engaged by the threat-detection system. In this example the individual would be reclassifying himself as an ingroup member, so displacing to another, common outgroup the prejudice that might otherwise be directed towards him.

Another strategy is *integration*. Individuals who choose this path, who maintain their original sense of identity while also sharing that of the host society, and are adept at dealing with both cultures, are *bicultural*. I've noted already that when people are encouraged to integrate it has been shown to be the most successful strategy for promoting positive intercultural relations, as well as revealing a qualitatively different psycho-logical system from the default tendency to separate the world into 'us' and 'them'. It is this alternative system that demon-strates the importance of coalitional thinking in modern behavioural experiments.

Bicultural individuals maintain their original sense of iden-tity while also sharing the host society's. In other words, they have adapted by integrating their conflicting cultural identities. Research suggests there may be broader cognitive benefits accruing from these individuals' experience of cultural diver-sity. For a start, they come to understand conflicting cultural assumptions and use this knowledge to think and behave appropriately in relevant contexts. This ability tends to facilitate communication and integration with both cultures, so that bicultural individuals are able to construe people, objects and ideas in a less rigid, stereotypical way than people who have internalised only one culture – precisely the evidence for enhanced cognitive abilities predicted by the Evolutionary Contact Hypothesis.

There is some empirical evidence to support these assertions. In one study, Mexican-American and Anglo-American mothers were presented with vignettes describing a family in which a child had behavioural problems and were asked to explain the behaviour.[52] The researchers found that the bicultural Mexican-American mothers were significantly more 'perspectivistic' in their analysis of the behaviour than were the Anglo-American mothers. Specifically, they were more likely to explain the behaviour by identifying the interacting roles of environmental and psychological influences rather than picking on a single cause. Veronica Benet-Martínez and colleagues asked Anglo-American (monocultural) and Chinese-American (bicultural) college students to write ten statements describing either American culture, Chinese culture or, in the control condition, natural landscapes. They found that the biculturals' descriptions contained more words and more distinct ideas, were more likely to discuss time-related and dynamic trends, and were more abstract, referring more to cultural values than to physical entities like food and sport.[53] They also drew on multiple perspectives in which different ideas were compared and contrasted, rather than relying on the first, dominant, responses that came to mind.

While this research on biculturals is compelling, there is another area of modern cross-cultural psychology that provides even stronger evidence that intercultural contact can stimulate advanced cognitive abilities. This is from research on the psychology of creativity.

CREATIVITY

Creativity is the ability to 'think outside of the box'. It is critical for problem-solving, progress, change and innovation. It helps people to achieve great scientific feats, invent ingenious gadgets, forge companies and careers, paint beautiful paintings and attract potential partners. It generates innovation and kick-starts success.

The good news is that creativity is not some genetic quirk of nature, a God-given gift bestowed on just the lucky few. Scientific studies have begun to reveal the anatomy of this ethereal skill. We now know a great deal about the psychological processes that drive creative cognition, and most importantly, the conditions that enable it to be captured, cultivated, developed and grown. This work provides a tantalising insight into the conditions that, if harnessed, could help us all fulfil our creative potential.

The ability to put aside existing knowledge and beliefs, to go beyond the everyday, mentally accessible ways of thinking, is perhaps the most established component of creativity and innovation. In contrast, when people over-rely on existing knowledge it constrains their capacity for flexible and innovative thought and perpetuates reliance on norms and conventions.

Creativity is the essence of advanced cognition – it is what the human brain does best, the pinnacle of cognitive evolution.

It is everything that we have been talking about in this book. And it involves exactly those cognitive capabilities that evolved to enable our ancestors to build intercultural bridges. Coalitional thinking requires the ability to inhibit existing ideas such as stereotypes and fear of outgroups. Coalitional thinking enables us to envisage things as different from how they are now, to generate alternative realities and prospects for the future. Working together with a previously feared outgroup and envisaging how a coalition could work is a good example of this kind of thinking. These are the critical elements of the cognitive capabilities our ancestors needed to build intergroup coalitions – and they are precisely the processes identified by modern cognitive science as central to creativity.

If creativity has its origins in our ancestors' need to think differently and innovatively about intercultural contact, then we should see a correlation between intercultural contact and creativity in modern behavioural science. One area in which this has been observed is in studies of bilingualism. By learning a second language, typically representative of a host culture, bilinguals have demonstrated a clear motivation to cognitively engage with the process of cultural integration. Bilinguals typically score higher on verbal-creativity tests than their monolingual counterparts.

One study compared Mexican high school students who were either Spanish-English bilingual or Spanish monolingual.[54] This study found that the bilinguals scored significantly higher than the Spanish monolinguals on the Torrance Tests of Creative Thinking, in terms of fluency and originality as well as flexibility. A study comparing Russian-English bilingual student immigrants living in the US and Russian-English bilingual university students living in Russia to monolingual English native speakers found that the bilinguals outperformed the other groups on tests of creative thinking and in measures of divergent-thinking abilities. They were better able to simultaneously activate multiple unrelated concepts and to keep them active during the thought process.[55] Many other studies have demonstrated that bilingualism is associated with this sort of enhanced cognitive performance.

While bilingualism may typically accompany intercultural contact, the two need not go together – you could learn another language in your bedroom without ever meeting anyone from the relevant culture! So we cannot safely conclude from these studies that intercultural contact produces uplifts in creative cognition. We can, however, from studies that have directly compared creative performance in those who have spent time abroad to control groups who have not.

CONTACT AND CREATIVITY

Building social relations and overcoming group differences was the essential element in a social ecosystem that enabled our ancestors' intellectual evolution – that's the idea I've outlined so far in this book. I'm now going to suggest that this Evolutionary Contact Hypothesis has significant implications not just for our understanding of how the human mind evolved, but also for how we can harness these abilities in the modern world. There is growing evidence that one particular activity is incredibly useful for stimulating this social brain system – travelling abroad.

Some of the most compelling research comes from longitudinal studies tracking people who had lived abroad for a year.

This work demonstrates the causal relationship between those experiences and creative thinking.

In one study, researchers gave a creativity test to MBA students on the same course who had either just returned from a study year abroad or had opted not to take it.[56] The task the students undertook is called the Duncker candle problem – it's a classic cognitive-performance test. The participant is required to solve a seemingly simple problem. He or she is presented with a candle, a box of matches and a box of tacks, and is required to fix the lit candle to a wall so that wax won't drip onto the floor. Many who do this test fail, attempting either to fix the candle to the wall using just the tacks, or to melt some of the wax and try to use it as an adhesive – neither method works. These responses demonstrate the cognitive miser in operation – a reliance on norms and conventions. They also reveal 'functional fixedness' – the inability to see a non-typical use for objects. The *creative* solution is to empty the box of tacks, put the candle in the box and use the tacks to nail the box, containing the candle, to the wall. This is thinking out of the box (literally!) – seeing that the box of tacks can be separated into two functional components and used to solve the task. Critically, the correct creative solution was obtained more often by the MBA students who had just returned from a year abroad than by those who hadn't.

Similarly, when European-American undergraduates watched a 45-minute slide show focusing just on Chinese culture (a unicultural context), or on American and Chinese culture (a juxtapositional context), or on elements of American-Chinese fusion culture (a fusional context) or on American culture (the control context), participants performing in the juxtapositional and fusional contexts wrote more creative stories than those performing in the other two contexts.[57] Other studies have measured intercultural contact using a question-naire inventory. Items measured family immigration history, length of time spent outside the participants' home state, foreign-language competency, the ethnicity of their closest friends and favourite musicians or groups, and the kinds of cuisine served in their favourite restaurants. Those with higher scores on this scale showed greater fluency in generating creative ideas.[58]

Evidence can also be found in historical accounts of culture and creativity. Archival analysis has found that in Japan's history the number of eminent individuals in a generation was a positive function of the amount of foreign influence in the culture.[59] Other analyses have suggested that warfare depresses creative output, as does anarchy, assassinations and coups d'état.[60] On the other hand, when a civilisation is diverse – fragmented into a number of peacefully coexisting independent states – this appears to boost the innovations emerging from that culture.[61] Interestingly, revolt against empires tends to lead to more creativity in subsequent generations. Rebellion encourages cultural diversity, but also the inhibition of current norms and thinking about how things could be different.

CULTURE BROADLY DEFINED

So far we have described intercultural contact as involving groups that differ in terms of what most people would regard as culture – ethnicity, race and religion. However, it is possible to define culture more broadly. Just as Western societies are becoming more multicultural, the boundaries that once defined categories such as gender, age, disability and sexuality are being slowly but surely eroded. Cultural difference can be defined by a range of different social roles and identities.

Evidence of the predicted relationship between intercultural contact and creative cognition may therefore be seen in a range of domains, most notably from studies of workplace diversity. For instance, research on diversity and workplace performance has defined diversity, broadly, as a construct that includes demographic (such as race and age) and non-demographic (educational, work experience and expertise) factors. It has been shown that when top management teams in the airline industry have been diverse in terms of education and expertise, they demonstrated a greater propensity for innovation than did more homogeneous teams.[62] Similar findings have been found in the textile industry.[63]

Exposure to minority viewpoints has also been found to stimulate divergent thinking – the kind of thinking that looks beyond obvious answers to problems. Working groups comprising many minorities tend to encourage and generate divergent thoughts and new ideas.[64] Exposure to alternative viewpoints also creates conflict and demands effort to resolve that conflict. As individuals typically adopt majority opinions much more quickly than minority ones, taking a minority viewpoint will involve a longer period of conflict and, accordingly, greater cognitive effort, as well as more issue-relevant and in-depth information processing. People considering a minority opinion will pay attention to more aspects of the situation, engage in more divergent thinking, and stand a greater chance of detecting novel solutions and coming to new decisions than those exposed to majority viewpoints.

Studies have shown that participants exposed to a minority group's problem-solving attempts came up with more novel solutions in a subsequent task than did participants exposed to a majority group's efforts. Similarly, mock juries forced to come to a unanimous decision, and so having to consider minority viewpoints, tended to consider evidence in more detail and take longer to reach their decision than juries who were only required to come up with a majority decision.[65] Such divergent thinking has been shown to be an essential element of creativity, involving as it does an individual's exposure to numerous alternatives and the chance to explore connections between them.

COGNITIVE DEVELOPMENT

Although initially thought to apply to immigrants' behaviour in adapting to the social and cultural demands of a host society, acculturation strategies, it is now recognised, apply both to immigrants and to the indigenous – often majority – host members. In other words, acculturation is relevant not only to those who are the source of that diversity – that is, *being* of another culture – but also to the majority group members who *perceive* that other culture. Any exposure to different cultures should stimulate the coalitional brain system, and in turn creative cognition. Research in developmental psychology shows just this.

Children vary in the extent to which they develop the capacity to understand that the same person can belong to two social groups simultaneously. Very young pre-schoolers typically have difficulty sorting people along a single social dimension; for example, they cannot sort a series of pictures of children according to gender or hair colour. Older pre-school children tend to be able to sort people along one dimension – for example, according to gender – but not along a second dimension at the same time (say, according to gender *and* hair colour). What this means is that young children find it difficult – if not impossible – to imagine that a person could belong to more than one distinct group at the same time. If, for example, an individual is 'a woman' and also 'an engineer', they may only be able to see her as a woman. Again, because they have difficulty processing more than one category, they may find it hard to understand that the individual can be both a woman *and* an engineer. On the other hand, if the individual being pro- cessed by the child is 'a man' and 'an engineer', because the second category fits into the male stereotype it is more likely to be successfully processed by the younger child despite his or her inability to classify on more than one dimension. The reason is that the socially prescribed attributes of men and engineers overlap to such an extent that they have become effectively just one category.

Developmental changes gradually enable children to classify objects into increasingly sophisticated categories. The onset of the concrete operational stage at the age of seven leads to the development of multiple classification skills. At this stage, children no longer view category membership as exclusive, and are able to understand that objects may fall along two or more dimensions simultaneously. If children can process informa- tion revealing that an individual is both a 'woman' and an 'engineer' they are likely to have less rigid stereotypes about women, because their improved classification skills allow them to process information that doesn't support the stereotype.

Interestingly, however, researchers have shown that it is possible to train children to classify along multiple dimensions, and therefore accelerate their developmental trajectory. In one study[66] children aged between five and ten were shown pictures of men and women engaging in stereotypically feminine (hairstylist, secretary) and stereotypically masculine (construction worker, truck driver) occupations. The children practised sorting these pictures according to both gender *and* occupation simultaneously, over several weeks. Competence at multiple classification over the training period increased from 3 per cent to 95. Moreover, successfully trained children showed significantly less gender stereotyping, and a better memory for counter-stereotypical gender information, than those who had not acquired multiple-classification skills.

What is important about this research is that the training essentially involved exposing children to cultural diversity, where culture is defined as the culture of work and the gender roles that are conventionally associated with different occupations. That they were found to have developed greater cognitive flexibility following this form of intercultural contact supports the Evolutionary Contact Hypothesis. It also has significant practical implications for education. Opponents of policies promoting multiculturalism argue that focusing on diversity in schools takes attention away from their true purpose – to foster academic excellence – because the former is achieved at the expense of the latter. The research I've just described stands in direct contravention of these views, suggesting that diversity is a critical component of academic attainment.

This, in turn, suggests that diversity should be fostered in schools not only as personal and social education, but as a key component of cognitive-skills training.

One final important thing to note is that the sort of training outlined above has also been found to promote creativity in adults. In my own research[67] I've asked participants to form impressions of a 'woman' who is also an 'engineer' – an example of 'intercultural' contact in the gender and occupation domains. The participants were then asked to generate three new names for pasta, and were given five examples (all made-up names). All the examples ended with the letter 'i', but those taking part in the study were never explicitly told that they should copy any of the examples' features. Flexibility (meaning here, the ability to ignore easily accessible information) was measured by computing the number of new pasta names participants generated that did not end with an 'i'. They were also asked to develop a novel idea for a themed event that could be held at the university nightclub; they were first asked to develop their idea in writing, then to sketch a poster advertising it. Two coders who were unaware of which experimental condition participants had been allocated to, or the hypotheses of the experimenter, judged the creativity of the ideas and the posters. Both of these measures revealed significant increases in creativity resulting from the intercultural-contact exercise. This work suggests that it is indeed possible to create social contexts and experiences that trigger our coalition-building system, and in turn to generate creative and flexible approaches to problem-solving exercises.

SUMMARY

If humans originally evolved advanced cognitive abilities as a direct result of cooperative intergroup contact, then those same social conditions should activate coalitional thinking in modern humans. A growing body of research supports this Evolutionary Contact Hypothesis and the idea that intercultural contact does, literally, broaden the mind. The ability to put aside existing knowledge and beliefs, to go beyond established and mentally accessible ways of thinking, is a key component of creativity and innovation. Research in a range of different domains, and using an array of methodologies, does indeed reveal that creative performance can be fostered by inter-cultural contact. In contrast, when people rely on stereotypes and don't venture to understand or engage with different cultures, their capacity for flexible and innovative thought is constrained and a reliance on norms and conventions is promoted.

This work supports the notion that intercultural contact was the essential element that made our ancestors' intellectual evolution possible. The significance, reach and potential impact of this relationship cannot be understated, as it offers us a new psychological model to explain how complex societies form, develop, prosper and grow.

In the next two chapters I delve deeper into the specific cognitive mechanisms that make up this coalition-building system, then speculate on the broader potential that harnessing this system could have for individuals, groups, governments and society at large.

CHAPTER 7

THE POWER OF PROSPECTION

In the preceding chapters I have argued that our ancestors developed a cognitive system specifically designed to enable them to tackle the most challenging (social) ecological problem they faced: the need to de-escalate inter-tribal conflict, and establish positive intergroup relations. I've argued that critical cognitive tools like the ability to see the other person's perspective, and to imagine things being different from how they are, evolved to enable positive intercultural contact to flourish and, in turn, provide the building-blocks of a cohesive, adaptive and diverse society.

According to this account, as the human population reached a tipping point and groups could no longer avoid contact with each other, they had two choices: compete, or cooperate. Competition and conflict presented one strategy, and one that was likely successful for stronger groups. Indeed, many evolutionary psychologists have proposed that competition and conflict were such a defining characteristic of our ancestors' habitat that threat-based systems of stereotyping and prejudice became hardwired from here on. However, I've argued that adapting to intergroup contact was just as important for the evolution of social cognition. In particular, the ability to form coalitions and ever larger collectives would ultimately have been more adaptive than constant competition and conflict. Indeed, if conflict had been the only way to deal with inter-cultural relations it is difficult to see how the human race could have developed beyond localised inter-tribal spats. The proposed coalitional-brain system would have been a critical step towards building a bigger society. Human adaptation to cultural diversity may have ultimately been more influential in shaping civilisation than any other single factor alone.

And yet conflict remains pervasive in the modern world – the default position in intercultural relations. Socio-culturally this does make evolutionary sense. We know our ancestors were more likely to survive in a dangerous world if they assumed, at first, that outgroupers would be dangerous. In contrast, all the evidence for coalitional thinking is gleaned from studies where the participants had *no choice* but to engage in intercultural contact. These include studies of biculturals or immigrants, or studies where experimental tasks specifically required coalitional thinking. For our ancestors, sheer necessity – having to pool inter-tribal resources so as to survive famine or a common aggressor, for instance – may have demanded such thinking. But what about in the modern world? If the system always defaults to an assumed threat, then prejudice will pervade and the benefits of coalitional thinking will remain elusive.

This presents something of a 'diversity paradox'. On the one hand the research suggests we need intercultural contact for our societies and minds to develop, progress and grow. Yet the prospect of intercultural contact is the very thing that compels us to avoid other groups, consigning us to conservative modes of thinking designed to protect and defend, not to explore and grow.

How then to overcome outgroup avoidance? Psychological scientists have claimed that to understand what guides behaviour we need to reach into the mind's 'cognitive toolbox' and jump-start the key systems. It's a bit like trying to figure out why your car won't start. The ignition button may no longer work, but the mechanic can go under the bonnet and get it going manually. A not dissimilar approach can be used to directly access the benefits of coalitional thinking. To extend the analogy: if the system has broken down, we need to open the bonnet and ignite the sparkplug. That process of reaching under the hood of the social brain, and stimulating the coalition-building system, is the focus of this chapter.

OVERCOMING THE URGE TO AVOID

To start with, let's delve deeper into the things that disincline people towards intercultural contact: those things that make threat detection and outgroup avoidance the default way of thinking for the modern mind. In Chapter 1 I described some key events of the twentieth century that have come to define intercultural contact and conflict. These events are precisely the sort of shared social experiences that compel people to eschew diversity – and the events we experience shape, focus and determine the way we think.

For instance, archival evidence has shown that economic downturns correlate with aggression and prejudice towards vulnerable targets such as minority groups. Take as an example the correlation between the price of cotton and the lynchings of African Americans between 1882 and 1930.[68] The case of the

2001 Bradford race riots suggests that poverty, deprivation and disillusionment were contributing factors. Anthropological studies have shown that conflict has been found to be greater amongst tribal groups who lived in close proximity to one another *and* competed for locally scarce resources like grazing land and water.[69] Behavioural experiments support the proposition that deprivation precipitates the avoidance of outgroups. They've shown that when teams have succeeded, everyone is equally popular. When they've failed, it was the minority co-workers who were blamed. In other words, when everything's going well diversity seems to be tolerated, but when resources become scarce, it's society's minorities who get the blame.

Then there's the threat from international terrorism. An established relationship between Islamic terrorism and anti-Muslim sentiment exists that parallels that observed in the case of economic hardship. Terrorism strikes a deep psychological chord, bringing to mind thoughts of our own mortality and, in turn, our capacity to live on through our culture. People adopt a range of religious beliefs, norms and worldviews to 'manage' this existential terror. Social systems, conventions and rules provide certainty and comfort to buffer our subconscious from this terror. Our cultures, and the view of the world they represent, allow us to psychologically transcend death – either through a belief in an afterlife, or symbolically, through lasting cultural achievements. They provide a sense of meaning and help us maintain a belief that our lives are significant.

Again, behavioural studies show that religious intolerance increases immediately after people are asked to contemplate their own death. Acts of terror, by their nature, bring forth thoughts of one's own eventual death, which then trigger behaviours designed to bring certainty, structure and coherence back to one's world. From this perspective, it's hardly surprising that when constantly bombarded with images of terrorist attacks, people react by raising society's drawbridge. Diversity delivers uncertainty and instability, the antithesis of what we need to counter the existential terror experienced at reminders of our own mortality. These trends show that terror and economic downturns trigger a psychological 'closing of ranks' – a desire to protect the ingroup tribe.

I've also discussed the process of acculturation, how when people successfully acculturate – that is, move to a new culture and integrate it with their existing viewpoints and norms – this can stimulate the development of greater cognitive flexibility. But what about the people who *don't* successfully acculturate? It's clear that many communities fail to integrate, preferring to keep themselves separate from the mainstream culture. One cause of this is the experience of discrimination and 'accultural stress'.[70] Immigrants will attempt to integrate their original cultural identity with that of their host country only when motivated to do so. It's therefore not surprising that those who experience high levels of discrimination prefer separation over integration, and will be disinclined to embrace integration strategies.

Some social scientists argue that the conflict resulting from attempting to reconcile opposing behavioural norms may not be cognitively beneficial, but associated with a range of negative outcomes including frustration, distress, uncertainty, anxiety, depression, marginalisation, insecurity, guilt and fear, along with a general depreciation of well-being and self-esteem. As well as coping with discrimination and racism, having to deal with the conflict between the two sets of values, attitudes and ways of life – those of their native culture and those of the host society – can be extremely stressful. Where original and host cultures are not incompatible, accultural stress will not arise and assimilation will occur. However, where people's different cultural 'frames' conflict (in terms of norms, ideologies and worldviews) there will be the potential for negative outcomes. Individuals may simply choose to ignore one of the two frames and withdraw entirely. This means that even when the opportunity to engage in contact is apparent, it can have varied psychological or behavioural impacts.

But it's not just discrimination that can lead people to shy away from the challenge of integrating two identities. The degree to which an individual feels intercultural contact is personally relevant is important. Diversity is usually personally relevant to people entering a new host culture by virtue of their minority status. Accordingly, immigrants might be expected to be more motivated to embrace integration than their majority host. Furthermore, for anyone contemplating a greater engagement with diversity there are a number of factors that may affect her or his motivation. Individual differences in a personality characteristic called 'need for cognition' can reduce people's desire to engage in intercultural contact. 'Openness to experience' is another personality variable that has a bearing on the likelihood of people seeking out and embracing challenging experiences – intercultural contact is precisely that sort of experience.

People with a strong need for what's referred to as 'cognitive closure' may be less influenced by exposure to diversity. Such individuals prefer order and predictability, and tend to be decisive and not very open-minded; they would rather be given firm answers than have to consider multiple alternatives. If the norms of their own particular culture provide conventional and widely accepted solutions, research shows that people with a high need for cognitive closure will tend to use those norms to guide their judgements. For instance, if asked to give examples of fruit, they are particularly likely to list apples and oranges rather than rarer fruits like kiwi fruit or tomatoes. Having a high need for cognitive closure can be a factor that predisposes individuals against engaging in coalitional thinking during intercultural contact.

Ideologies – defined as complex webs of attitudes and values – can also affect whether people embrace diversity. A multicultural ideology is the belief that society should tolerate, include, and afford equal status to different religious, ethnic and cultural groups. Adopting a multicultural ideology is specifically relevant to the experience of social and cultural diversity, as we can assume that individuals who value diversity and difference will be motivated to engage in the process of resolving stereotypical inconsistencies.

However, all the things I've just mentioned are measures of individual difference – variations across individuals in any given population. They offer no way of encouraging people to tap into the coalitional system, no way to unleash the full power of their creative cognition. Diversity, in real life, may spawn a number of associated stressors that militate against intercultural contact. Low motivation may lead to stereotype-challenging diversity being perceived as threatening, stressful or aversive, leading to negative psychological or behavioural outcomes. This may be the case, for instance, when an immigrant experiences racial discrimination; or when someone experiences sexism on attempting to enter a profession typically associated with the other gender. Similarly, pressure to accept multiculturalism may threaten the identity of majority-group members, resulting in a reactive increase in bias in order to reassert group dominance in the same way that introducing a 'common ingroup' has been shown to increase bias amongst those who identify strongly with their own group. There are, then, a number of additional stressors that may impede individuals' efforts to adapt cognitively to their experiences of diversity.

From workplace studies, too, we see how difficult it is to trigger the coalition-building system in complex social contexts. When individuals from different groups are required to work together, this may not promote tolerance or open-mindedness but instead create social division that results in poor social integration, low cohesion levels and, accordingly, low-quality team performance. Similarly, unless individuals are motivated and able to resolve cultural conflict, stress and distress can result. In other words, differences that simply create divisions do *not* challenge expectations. Research in large organisations has found that demographic diversity in work groups can result in members being less psychologically attached to their group; they are typically less committed to remaining with the firm and have a higher level of absenteeism.[71]

These are all examples of what happens when categorical differences are merely *imposed* within an existing context. Rather than promoting cognitive flexibility, simply being aware of differences is likely to lead to the accentuation of category differentiation and intergroup bias. In contrast, groups are best at generating creative solutions when they require the *resolution* of cognitive conflict that emerges from diversity. Diversity should lead to increased performance because it results in the elaboration and exchange of information and the exchange of viewpoints. This brings with it deeper discussion and the integration of the information.

But in the absence of conditions that promote resolution this can generate intergroup bias. A critical factor is the motivation to engage in intercultural contact. Work groups must be motivated to think about their experience of diversity in a way that challenges existing expectations. It has been found that the benefits of work-group diversity are realised when group members are keen to resolve the 'fault lines' that will inevitably arise from time to time.[72] The same study suggests that diversity in work groups enhances output because the mental processes involved in bridging intercultural differences promote thinking styles that are key to good productivity and problem-solving. In particular, those mental processes lead to information being exchanged and different perspectives being adopted. This promotes, once again, deeper discussion and the integration of information.

However, for this scenario to be successful the climate must be one that encourages and enables positive intercultural communication – in other words, the broader organisational norms and ideologies should promote values that encourage intercultural communication. In addition, time pressure should be minimised to reduce the cognitive load and the tendency to fall back on stereotypes. In the absence of these conditions, diversity may lead to intergroup conflict. In short, there must be a willingness to challenge existing assumptions about cultures and to put stereotypical thinking aside.

As we can see, there's a multitude of factors that discline individuals to engage their coalitional brain and instead encourage them to rely on the easier threat-detection and outgroup-avoidance system. When diversity poses problems – whether because discrimination is being experienced or because individuals won't meet diversity halfway – people may simply ignore opportunities for intercultural contact. We need to kick-start their motivation, and to do this we must reach into the social brain's cognitive toolbox and access the coalition-building system. We need to artificially stimulate something called *prospection*.

PROSPECTION

Prospection is the capacity to mentally project oneself into the past or the future so as to consider alternative perspectives based on our past experiences. Being able to see into a range of possible futures is central to the human mind's ability to safely navigate the world. Think of all the accidents that could happen – a hand getting in the way of boiling water, tripping down-stairs – we avoid these because we can envisage the outcome.

The idea is that when we imagine a scenario in which we perform a particular action, a behavioural script will be formed and stored in our memory. When the script is recalled, it can then influence our expectations, intentions and interpretations of immediate events, as well as our behaviour in the situation at hand. Subsequently, when we are asked to make a judgement about intention, or perform the behaviour, the script will be available for use. Studies show that a wide range of judgements and beliefs are influenced by the mental availability of relevant information. Correspondingly, research has confirmed that once a behavioural script has been formed, through imagining the scenario, it influences one's expectations and intentions:

one now has mentally available a source of diagnostic knowledge that can be used to make judgements about one's
intentions. It is this ability to envisage different realities that
evolved as a key element of the coalitional-brain system.

Contemporary research in experimental psychology provides an illustration of how important this cognitive ability is
for everyday social interaction. Functional neuro-imaging has
shown that prospection uses the same neurological pathways
as are used in memory, motor control and, crucially, social
cognition.[73] In particular, the ability to imagine different
futures allows us to generate alternative outcomes for our past
behaviour. This is highly adaptive, as it enables us to review
our actions, see where we have gone wrong, and envisage an
alternative outcome. We can then project ourselves into the
future when we find ourselves in the same situation – in other
words, we can plan a better future for our actions.

This is called counterfactual thinking. Studies have shown
that in many cases, emotions regarding one's current situation
greatly depend on an imagined alternative reality that one can
generate.[74] 'Upward' counterfactual simulations – 'if only'
scenarios – involve the generation of alternatives that are better
than reality. They result from a negative outcome and decrease
one's satisfaction. 'Downward' counterfactual simulations – 'at
least' scenarios – involve imagining outcomes worse than
reality and can increase one's satisfaction with the outcome. In
terms of interpersonal negotiation, this scenario-building can
influence how people perceive and appraise their current situation and the risks and benefits that the future may bring.

The ability to review past behaviour and revise future plans
shows the functional overlap between memory and imagination. The overlap derives from the fact that memories of past

experience provide the foundation upon which alternative
futures can be conceived. Prospection is, therefore, not just
crucial to understanding others, it is crucial to the maintenance
of self-esteem; to helping us chart a way through the triumphs,
trials and tribulations of everyday life. It enables and empowers
our ambitions, aims and aspirations.

Research illustrates this fundamental function in the
rehearsal and planning of behaviour. In one study[75] undergraduate students were asked to either think about the reasons
why they should study – for instance, to learn new things, to
achieve better grades, boost self-confidence – or imagine the
actions they might take in order to effectively study – such as
create a comfortable atmosphere, work with a friend, reward
themselves. Imagining actions elicited more effective and productive study behaviours than did generating reasons.
Similarly, researchers have attempted to reduce psychotherapy-
course dropout rates at an outpatient clinic by using a scripted
simulation procedure administered at the intake session.[76]
Those who imagined staying in therapy reported an increased
expectancy of staying there, and were less likely to drop out
subsequently.

There are many other examples of the use of prospection in
a whole range of other domains. In sport it has been observed
that runners who imagine running faster can then literally run
faster. Weight-lifters who imagine lifting a heavier weight
seem to succeed in doing so.[77] Imagery is also used extensively
in the treatment of phobias and anxiety disorders. It works by
gradually exposing patients to the object or situation that
causes the phobia until it becomes tolerated. Imagined
exposure to the phobia-inducing stimuli is found to significantly
reduce anxiety and fear-related behaviours and emotions.[78]

Imagery can therefore quash our fears and overcome what are sometimes crippling psychological states.

What is important about all this is that it suggests prospection may also be key to the coalitional-brain system. So, just as people use behavioural scripts for a wide range of everyday scenarios – queuing, parking, visiting a restaurant – they seem also to equip themselves with intercultural communication scripts. In other words, as with any other action, prospection can allow people to imagine intercultural relationships as being different from how they currently are. Evidence for this assertion comes from a range of studies that have explored humans' capacity for *social* prospection: that is, the planning, rehearsal and enacting of interactions with others. Prospection provides, most pertinently, the ability to mentally time-travel that is necessary to transcend people's evolved tendencies to see outgroups as 'them', and to see a possible future in which they are also 'us'.

If prospection is indeed a central component of the coalitional system it should be possible to directly stimulate the mechanism by means of directed-imagery techniques. In the next chapter I'll discuss social psychological research that has done just this – harnessed the power of prospection to promote more positive intercultural relations.

SUMMARY

How to overcome outgroup avoidance? A core component of the coalitional brain is prospection – the ability to mentally project oneself into the past or the future to consider alternative realities. This ability is crucial to normal cognitive functioning. It helps us review our actions, see where we have made mistakes, and imagine an alternative outcome. With respect to building bonds in interpersonal communication, prospection allows us to overcome distrust and avoidance. Research in a range of areas shows how directly stimulating prospection processes can enhance our capacity to achieve goals, whether they be academic, professional, sporting or health-related. This work provides a compelling basis for the proposition that direct stimulation of the prospection system may also promote positive outcomes in intercultural communication.

CHAPTER 8

CONTACT RE-IMAGINED

As it turns out, there is a great deal of evidence for the use of prospection in human perception. Indeed, prospection has been right up there as a principal process of thinking since the first ever studies in experimental psychology, carried out by William James in 1890. However, what provides the most compelling evidence for the role of prospection in coalition thinking comes from new research on intergroup contact.

As discussed in Chapter 4, over five hundred studies have now confirmed that direct contact between groups can reduce prejudice and improve intercultural communication. But what if contact is prevented, by either physical or psychological barriers? Think about the most pervasive conflicts around the world – they are defined by separation and segregation. These barriers are not just physical, like the West Bank wall in Israel or the Green Line in Cyprus. They are also more implicit, like the lack of mixed Catholic–Protestant schools in Northern Ireland or the low percentage of mixed black–white neigh-bourhoods in the US. Even where physical segregation is not apparent, people have a tendency to coalesce around racial, religious or ethnic commonalities, thus creating de facto segregation. This self-categorisation process is the threat-detection system at work, serving to discourage intercultural contact even when the opportunity for it exists.

How, then, to tackle this pervasive problem of physical, social and psychological segregation?

Imagined intergroup contact[79] is a technique I've developed that involves mentally articulating an interaction between different cultures and groups. It is a way of directly accessing the prospection system, simulating and stimulating an interest in intercultural contact (or intergroup contact more generally). It provides a real way of accessing the benefits of contact where there is no other means of doing so. Perhaps more importantly, it overcomes the threat-detection system, countering self-imposed segregation. It provides a way of resolving the diversity paradox outlined in the preceding chapter.

In practical terms, imagined contact involves the mental simulation of possible future interactions with members of the outgroup. For instance, people can be encouraged to think about everyday situations in which they might run into individuals from different cultures (on the bus, at the supermarket). They can think about what the person is wearing, whether he or she is alone or with friends or family. Most importantly, they can think about the conversation they have, what they learn, how they feel, and how the experience could change their view of the group in question.

I have found that engaging in this kind of social prospection – that is, running through the behavioural script of an intercultural interaction – can have a significant impact on attitudes. This is because it provides people with a positive mental script for what to expect in intercultural contact. In so doing it reduces anxiety and promotes a positive interest in diversity.

For instance, in my initial test of the Imagined Contact Hypothesis, my lab conducted a series of studies[80] in which the participants were asked to imagine encountering an outgroup member before reporting their attitudes towards the outgroup in general. Specifically, we asked the student participants (who were aged around eighteen to twenty-one) to spend a minute imagining a positive interaction with an elderly stranger. Participants in the control condition were asked to imagine an outdoor scene instead. After writing down what they had imagined, they were told about a future study in which they could *interact* in person with either an elderly person or a fellow young person. They were then asked to indicate which of these two interaction partners they would prefer. While participants in the control condition were biased in favour of conversing with other young people, those who had previously imagined interacting with an elderly person were equally happy to interact with either of the proposed partners.

In subsequent studies we have shown that imagined contact can improve attitudes towards a range of groups, including Muslims, immigrants and asylum seekers. We have even found that this direct stimulation of the prospection system can counteract the hardwired millisecond-level biases described in Chapter 3. For instance, in one study[81] participants were asked either to imagine contact with an elderly person or, in a control condition, to imagine an outdoor scene. Implicit bias was measured using the Implicit Association Test. This reaction-time task asked participants to categorise 'young' names like Brad, Zack and Lucy, and 'elderly' names like Cyril, Arthur and Mildred, alongside positive words like 'smile' and 'paradise' and negative words like 'slime' and 'pain'. In the control condition we found the typical bias in favour of ingroup (young) positive associations and outgroup (elderly) negative associations. After imagining contact, though, this difference in reaction times was eliminated.

In the next study, non-Muslim participants imagined a contact experience with a British Muslim. We again used the IAT, but this time the young and elderly names were replaced with typical Muslim names such as Mohammed, Fatima and Yusra, and non-Muslim names like Matthew, Luke and Eve. In the control condition there was the typical associative bias for ingroup and positive / outgroup and negative word-name pairings. After imagining contact, however, this bias was completely eliminated. Imagined contact had effectively 'switched off' the threat-detection system.

These findings are especially important because millisecond biases are indicative of subtle non-verbal behaviours in everyday interactions. Such behaviours serve to maintain self-segregation even in apparently egalitarian societies. Using prospection to tackle these implicit biases may have a significant knock-on effect, producing smoother intercultural communication in future.

ENCOURAGING INTERACTIONS

Imagined contact can improve attitudes and make people more confident about their ability to engage in contact with outgroup members, should the situation arise. But could directly stimulating prospection help encourage people to actively seek out more intercultural contact?

In other areas of behavioural science it is established that prospection encourages intention. Recall the study where students were directed either to think about the reasons why they should find studying enjoyable (such as learning new things, making better grades, boosting self-confidence) or to imagine what they might *do* to make it more enjoyable – create a comfortable atmosphere, study with a friend, reward oneself. The researchers found that imagining what they might actually do (rather than simply generating reasons) was the most effective way of encouraging them to study.

I've found that imagined contact can elicit similarly enhanced intentions to engage in intercultural contact. In one study,[82] British non-Muslim students were asked to imagine contact with a British Muslim, or were allocated to a control condition. On a measure of intentions, the participants who imagined contact reported greater intentions to engage in future contact than did participants in the control condition.

A related question is whether imagined contact can also increase people's confidence in their intercultural-communication ability – without, for instance, inadvertently displaying behaviours that could be construed as prejudiced. This kind of 'self-efficacy' is a key determinant of people's willingness to engage in a specific behaviour. If they are not confident in their ability to successfully negotiate the task in hand, their incentives to act are limited. Enhancing confidence in their intercultural-communication skills would yield con-siderable benefits for intercultural relations.

Again, research in other areas of behavioural science suggests that prospection enhances self-efficacy. As described above, in sports-psychology studies it's been observed that participants who imagined themselves lifting a heavy object became more confident in their ability to lift heavier weights. Similar effects have been observed for imagined intercultural

contact. In one study[83] my lab found that non-Muslim participants who imagined contact with British Muslims, afterwards
endorsed more strongly statements such as 'I would feel confident talking to British Muslims' and 'I would feel I have
common topics for conversation with British Muslims.'

These studies demonstrate that as well as changing attitudes,
imagining intercultural contact can increase confidence in dealing with such contact when it occurs. Enhancing self-efficacy
is an important part of the process of orienting people more
positively towards intercultural contact, making them feel confident that they will act appropriately, and without bias.
However, confidence is not action, and what we really need to
know is whether imagined contact can enhance actual intercultural communication.

READY, WILLING – BUT ABLE?

So stimulating prospection can promote confidence, self-
efficacy and positive intention. Are these then translated into
behaviour? As mentioned earlier, non-verbal behaviour in
intercultural communication is important for fostering better
relations, and is likely to have the greatest impact on the success of the encounter. We know that while people tend to be
able to control conscious behaviour, such as the verbal content
of their speech (what they actually say) they struggle to hide
anxiety, which is usually displayed more subtly through non-
verbal behaviour in much the same way as millisecond-level
bias is conveyed. Non-verbal behaviour can profoundly affect
the success or otherwise of intercultural interactions: it can
mean the difference between forging a coalition and making an
enemy. If prospection is indeed a key component of an evolved

coalitional brain system, imagined contact should be able to elicit improved non-verbal communication.

Specifically, imagined contact should prepare people for intercultural communication by suppressing the negative non-verbal behaviours that might otherwise be elicited by being in the presence of the outgroup. It should smooth intercultural interactions via improved non-verbal skills. And the effect should snowball: past research shows that positive behaviour during such interactions tends to be reciprocated. The non-verbal expression of trust and liking will build trust and liking, and vice versa.

Some research from my lab directly tested this hypothesis. In the study participants were asked to record a video welcome message for international students joining their university. Following this, independent coders watched the videos and rated how fluent and friendly the participants' body language and speech were. We showed that, consistent with the principles outlined above, increased anxiety about intercultural contact led to poorer-quality communication.[84] But when the participants were asked to first carry out an imagined contact exercise, this negative relationship between anxiety and the fluency of communication was eliminated. In other words, imagining contact beforehand resulted in the participants demonstrating improved, positive body language and speech when they engaged in communicating.

EVIDENCE FROM EDUCATION

If imagined contact is a way of teaching us to use a latent social-prospection system, it should be effective in education. Two recent studies are notable in their attempt to test the effectiveness of imagined contact in this regard. In one study[85] able-bodied children aged between five and ten were asked to spend three minutes creating a story, using pictures and photographs, that featured themselves and a disabled child playing together in a park. Attitudes and behavioural intentions were then assessed through a structured interview. The researchers found that the participants who had imagined intergroup contact were subsequently more positive in their attitudes towards disabled people. Moreover, after the exercise they were more likely to want to be friends with disabled children.

In another study[86] Italian fifth-graders (aged around ten) were asked to imagine having a pleasant encounter with an unknown immigrant child who had just arrived in the country. To broaden the experiment, participants imagined contact with a different child each time and in a different context – school, neighbourhood or park. One week later a range of measures were taken, including a response-time Implicit Association Test and asking the children about their behavioural intentions. Specifically they were asked whether they would be happy to meet, play with, or have ice-cream with an immigrant child. The results revealed that those who had imagined contact over the preceding three sessions subsequently had more positive behavioural intentions and showed reduced millisecond-level bias.

Together the findings from these studies show that imagined contact can be successfully applied in educational settings. In addition, the effects were shown to last for up to a week, suggesting this kind of direct stimulation of the prospection system is quite powerful.

Finally, a recent study[87] carried out in Italy asked fifth-graders to participate in a three-week experiment that involved imagining meeting an unknown immigrant peer in various situations. A week after the last session, the researchers found that imagined contact had led to more positive attitudes and behaviour towards immigrants. These positive intergroup attitudes were then applied by the participants to similar out-groups. This suggests that cognitive interventions like imagined contact may ultimately promote more widespread tolerance in society.

OPTIMISING IMAGINED INTERACTIONS

In the research on imagined contact in educational settings, the imagery tasks were typically more involving and elaborate than in the early studies with adults. This makes sense, given what we know of the prospection system in the human brain, which works by mentally projecting the individual to a possible future when he or she will carry out the proposed action. The more detailed and elaborate that projection, the stronger will be the resulting behavioural script formed in the individual's mind.

Accordingly, in later research I've developed a kind of guided intercultural prospection that requires individuals to engage in a more detailed imagined encounter. This version of imagined contact directs the participants to imagine details such as when it might happen – next Thursday, say – and where – the bus stop. As well as the potential practical benefits of strengthening the effects of the imagined contact task, modifying it in this way enabled me to test the proposed under-lying behavioural-script mechanism. The reason why this sort of guided prospection should be more powerful is because it should provide a more precise cognitive roadmap for future behaviour.

In a study[88] carried out in my lab I reasoned that if guided intercultural prospection creates a more vivid, cue-rich script upon which to build plans about future intercultural relations, then these participants would predict having more outgroup friends in the future. The findings revealed just this: participants estimated that in five years' time they would have more outgroup friends after guided imagery than following the standard imagined contact procedure. Another study revealed that significantly stronger intentions to engage in future contact were reported by participants who engaged with the elaborated imagery procedure.

In this work the vividness of the imagined scenario was also measured. Vivid visual imagery has characteristics resembling the real scenario in that it is generally clear, bright, sharp, detailed and lively. It has been argued that anything that enhances the vividness of an imagined scenario should lead to the formation of stronger behavioural intentions because it is indicative of a concrete, cue-rich and available behavioural script. The vividness of the imagined scenario is a good indication of how available the formed script will be when participants come to make judgements.

In order to measure the vividness of the imagined scenarios the participants were asked the degree to which, according to the following dimensions, the image was faint–vivid, fuzzy–clear, dim–bright, vague–sharp, dull–lively, simple–detailed. The study revealed that the stronger intentions to engage in future contact were statistically explained by the enhanced vividness reported after the guided imagery procedure. These findings support the notion that creating a vivid, cue-rich contact scenario is an important process through which imagined contact exerts its positive effects.

Another way of optimising the impact of prospection is to manipulate the perspective taken. One of the advantages of the imagined-contact task is that it can be moulded to create the best possible conditions for contact to succeed, perhaps in ways that are difficult to achieve in more direct contact scenarios. If imagined contact creates a behavioural script that people can draw upon in making judgements about outgroups, it may be possible to make subtle modifications to how that script is formed that will have implications for how people see themselves in those encounters. For instance, it is possible to guide people in these exercises to take a first-person perspective; that is, to imagine the encounter 'through their own eyes'. Alternatively, people can be guided to take a third-person perspective; that is, to look down on themselves from a kind of 'bird's eye view'.

Recent research has shown that changing the imagined visual perspective in this way can impact on the effects of simulated behaviour. For instance, students asked to imagine preparing for an academic test from a third-person perspective reported a higher motivation for subsequent achievement compared to participants who imagined carrying out the task from a first-person perspective. Similarly, a group of US researchers asked respondents to picture themselves voting on the eve of the 2004 US presidential elections. They also instructed them to use either the first-person or third-person viewpoint. Those who pictured themselves voting from the third-person viewpoint adopted a stronger pro-voting attitude, corresponding with the imagined behaviour.

Taking a third-person perspective helps perceivers frame the imagined event in more abstract terms, and in terms of the broader significance it has for one's life. In contrast, taking a first-person perspective compels perceivers to frame the imagined events in more concrete terms, focusing on the emotions they experienced in that specific context. In other words, taking a first-person perspective might make concrete aspects of the situation salient – so the participant might conclude: 'This was a positive encounter with an outgroup member'. In contrast, taking a third-person perspective makes more abstract aspects salient – so the participant might conclude: 'I am an egalitarian person.' Because the latter has greater implications for one's sense of self, it should also have a correspondingly greater impact on subsequent behaviour.

To test whether this approach would also enhance the effects of intergroup prospection, my lab carried out a study.[89] We allocated sixty undergraduate participants to conditions in which they were asked to imagine either a control scenario (e.g. walking in the countryside) or positive contact with an elderly stranger from either a first-person perspective ('See the event through your own eyes') or a third-person perspective ('See the event from an external viewpoint'). Intentions were measured, as was the extent to which participants viewed themselves as having a positive orientation towards contact with the elderly. The kind of question asked was, 'In general, are you the sort of person who gets on well with elderly people?'

As expected, perspective made no difference in the non-relevant control condition. However, imagining intergroup contact from a third-person perspective enhanced future contact intentions to a greater extent than imagining the encounter from a first-person viewpoint. Furthermore, the effects were accompanied by an enhanced perception of oneself as egalitarian (e.g. 'I am the sort of person who gets on well with elderly people'). This supports the notion that a third-person perspective encourages people to view the imagined interaction in relation to their broader ideas about the sort of person they might be.

MEMORY AND IMAGINATION

The integration of memory and imagery within the prospection system is key to understanding its coalition-building function. From a functional perspective, memory drives the detection of outgroup threat, preventing engagement with outgroups who have been found to be aggressive or hostile in the past. Correspondingly, prior intercultural contact is one of the most robust predictors of intergroup anxiety, which has the effect of preventing engagement with outgroups about whom little is known. However, it also makes sense for memory to be tied into the prospection system because this enables the coalitional system to inhibit memories of negative outgroup encounters. Prospection, as we have seen, is about considering alternative realities that, by definition, have not yet happened. As such, the memory of past positive ingroup (or other outgroup) encounters may form the basis for a new simulation of a positive outgroup encounter. In building the imagined scenario, you can splice a memory of a previous positive encounter (with anyone – a friend, a family member or a stranger) into an imagined interaction with an outgroup member. In so doing you can acquire a positive contact script upon which you can base future judgements about the outgroup, and your own confidence in interacting with that outgroup. This self-efficacy can then be a driver of future intentions to engage in actual contact.

To build coalitions, individuals must project possible future interactions. Research has shown how imagery enables us to identify and organise the steps involved here, creating a plan of action. Correspondingly, imagining contact has been found to elicit enhanced intentions to engage in intergroup contact by increasing the cognitive availability of positive contact scripts, thereby reducing intergroup anxiety and enhancing self-efficacy in intergroup encounters.

As well as being able to plan the potential outcomes of inter-action with coalition partners, this process would be greatly aided by the ability to take another's perspective. Perspective-taking is inferring the internal psychological states of others; in other words, seeing the world through their eyes. It has been an integral component of diversity-training techniques developed by social psychologists. For instance, in one US study[90] the participants were asked to write an essay describing a day in the life of an African-American male or an elderly male. They then reported that they considered themselves to possess traits that were stereotypical of African-Americans or elderly males, respectively. By virtue of then feeling that they had more in common with the target person, the participants also developed more positive attitudes towards them.

A follow-up study found that perspective-taking led to more cooperative behaviour when target people lacked aggressiveness, but that it led to competition when they were stereotypically aggressive. Similarly, other research has shown that actively considering target people's perspective produced feelings of empathy and sympathy, leading the perspective-taker to offer greater assistance to them. It might therefore be the case that perspective-taking-induced empathy, in conjunc-tion with imagined positive contact, helps to strengthen future contact intentions. Collectively, planning, projection and perspective-taking can be considered key psychological capabilities that comprise the coalitional thinking system.

A NOTE ON LONGEVITY

There is an important caveat to the use of imagined contact that emerges from the research on intercultural experience and creativity discussed in Chapter 6. This showed that while useful for initiating a first step towards deeper intercultural interaction, vacations or short work trips, where the individual has little actual interaction with the host country's culture, customs and ideals, have little lasting impact on creativity. In other words, tapping into the broader benefits of intercultural communication is likely to be a long – possibly lifelong – process. It may begin with short, less involving trips, then in time the visits may become increasingly immersive, with individuals beginning to adopt a more integrative mindset. It's then that the broader benefits of intercultural experience may be realised.

This means that the sort of guided intercultural prospection exercises described in this chapter are unlikely to be a one-shot solution to promoting tolerance or enhancing cognitive flexibility. Instead, their value is in providing the first step on the road to fully accessing the cognitive benefits of the coalitional thinking system. For successful intercultural communication, individuals should then gradually engage with more and more immersive intercultural experiences, moving from a separate to an integrated ideological mindset – perhaps with the help of further guided-prospection techniques. When they achieve an integrative mindset they are most likely to have successful intercultural interactions that avoid conflict and challenge stereotypes. When this has been achieved, they may also enjoy enhanced and extended benefits in the form of greater creativity, problem-solving, resilience and cognitive flexibility. I will explore this process of intercultural immersion further in Chapter 9.

SUMMARY

In this chapter I've shown how a mental simulation technique called imagined contact can directly stimulate the coalition-building system. This form of intergroup prospection is crucial to the construction and rehearsal of responses to changing social conditions and, accordingly, it is integral to successful intercultural contact. Most importantly, I've argued that it is a key component of the coalitional system that our ancestors would have needed to effect positive change in intercultural relations: to build bridges and to envisage a future in which diverse groups could work together.

Modern behavioural science offers evidence for the key role of prospection in promoting more positive intercultural relations. Studies have shown that prospection, in the form of imagined intercultural contact, reduces prejudice and promotes intentions to engage in future contact. It reduces anxiety and elicits trust – two emotions that regulate both avoidance and engagement with outgroups. Research has also demonstrated how prospection enables individuals to identify and organise the steps involved in intended behaviour, creating a plan of action. Correspondingly, imagining an intercultural interaction has been found to increase the cognitive availability of positive contact scripts, enhance self-efficacy at the thought of future intercultural encounters, and increase the likelihood that those encounters will be successful. Collectively, this research supports the notion that directly stimulating prospection, the core component of the coalitional-brain system, can inhibit outgroup avoidance and promote positive relations.

CHAPTER 9

HOW TO MAKE A MODERN MIND

In this book the key proposition is that ecological changes in human prehistory led to a population tipping-point when our ancestors had a simple choice to make: conflict or cooperation? Some intercultural encounters would simply have triggered the default early-evolved, threat-focused cognitive system – a system that produces, ultimately, a propensity for conflict. However, it would not always have been adaptive to fight. Under some conditions the best survival option would have been to form a coalition. Those humans who could build bridges, overcome the inhibitions of outgroup avoidance and project a more positive picture of intergroup relations would therefore have gained a survival advantage. Those who possessed the power of prospection and other advanced cognitive abilities needed to negotiate peaceful relations would then have been 'selected' for evolutionary fitness.

Through this sociocultural lens we can see the origins of modern human cognition: the systems that enabled adaptation to social and cultural diversity. This suggests that there is an evolved coalition-building system that resides in the modern psyche – one that may be under-utilised but that offers profound potential. Identifying the social conditions that unlock this latent system may be key to triggering further great leaps in our development as a species.

I've argued that, advanced cognitive abilities like prospection evolved primarily as a means of building intercultural bridges. If this is the case we should be able to direct, exercise and develop that system by designing diversity training around the principles of prospection and intercultural contact. In the last chapter I described how imagined contact can help people prepare for intercultural interactions. In so doing, it enables individuals to access the benefits of flexible thinking and move beyond the default threat-focused, avoidant-thinking style. But this is only the first step – people then have to engage in actual intercultural contact in order to exercise the coalitional brain. In short, prospection on its own is not enough to unlock the potential embedded in intercultural contact – we need to design diversity training that goes beyond initial encounters and exercises all the cognitive components of coalitional thinking.

Based on the analysis I've provided in the preceding chapters and on what we know from contemporary intercultural-cognition research, we can map precisely the type of intercultural contact that should most effectively stimulate the coalitional thinking system, the stages through which consequent cognitive growth should progress, and the outcomes we should observe. Drawing on processes known to operate in different intercultural contexts, in this chapter I'll identify those contact characteristics that should most likely stimulate coalitional thinking. In so doing I'll describe a new model of intercultural adaptation[91] [92] [93] that specifies the conditions needed to stimulate cognitive growth, and the means by which it can be achieved.

KEY CONDITIONS

What kind of diversity experiences are most likely to activate the coalitional brain system? Three components are core. The first is what I'll call *immersion*. Recall that in Chapter 6 I described how research has demonstrated that individuals who had lived abroad, when asked to think about their living experiences there, subsequently performed better on a range of creativity tasks. For instance, they were more likely to correctly solve the Duncker candle-mounting problem – a measure of creativity, you'll remember, that requires inhibiting your knowledge about the customary uses of objects and thinking of new ones.

Importantly, this improvement in creativity was observed only if individuals had engaged in an *immersive* intercultural experience, such as living abroad for a year rather than merely having made a quick visit. Indeed, the more time participants had spent abroad, the more likely they were to solve the problem. More generally, across a wide spectrum of literature on creativity it's apparent that the effects of such experiences cannot be observed after a brief visit. There's something about living in a host culture and about the social, psychological and behavioural adjustments this requires that generates the kinds of creativity boost that have been observed in the scientific literature.

The second condition is *dual engagement*. As discussed earlier, acculturation describes the process via which immigrants moving to a new country psychologically react to their new social reality, a reality in which they must resolve potential conflicts between their original cultural identity and that of the new host nation. Studies have indicated that in order to acquire cognitive flexibility individuals must be motivated to engage with both host and home cultures. Put another way, they must adopt an integration mindset, actively trying to be part of both cultures, rather than an assimilation mindset, which would mean forgoing their former identity to adopt wholly the host culture. They should also not adopt a separation mindset which would entail maintaining their original identity and not engaging with the host culture.

When individuals become bicultural in this way, their creativity and mental flexibility are enhanced. For instance, as we saw in Chapter 6, it has been found that Chinese-American biculturals' descriptions of the Chinese and American cultures were more likely to include multiple perspectives in which different ideas were compared and contrasted than the first things that came to mind. Biculturals have also been found to possess higher levels of *integrative complexity* – the capacity and willingness to acknowledge the legitimacy of competing perspectives on an issue, and to forge conceptual links amongst those perspectives.

The acculturation literature, then, focuses on understanding the experience of immigrants; but it's the basic principles – how people deal with diversity – that can help us define the conditions that should stimulate the coalitional system. Engagement with both home and host cultures is one of the defining characteristics of long-term intercultural experience. In contrast to immigrants, long-term sojourners will be returning home some day and so are likely to be motivated to maintain a sense of their own culture (ruling out assimilation). We can therefore predict that in order for the coalitional thinking system to be activated during intercultural contact, the individual must be motivated to integrate her existing cultural perspective with that of the other group. In other words, she must engage with both cultural perspectives.

Finally, when it comes to dual engagement, not all diversity experiences are equal. Most importantly, groups can differ psychologically in terms of *cultural distance*. Cultural distance is the degree to which the values, customs and characteristics of different cultures diverge. Imagine a Brit spending a year in the USA. She will probably not face as many conflicts in customs, values and ideas as a Brit spending a year in China. If cultural distance is minimal, it is easy to engage with both cultures; in fact, the similarities between them may be so unchallenging that de facto assimilation occurs. With minimal cultural distance, dual engagement makes no real difference to how one has to think about the new situation because the two cultures converge so much. And without the experience of tangible cultural differences, plus the inevitable difficulty in dealing with those differences, there can be no cognitive development. In short, intercultural contact *has* to be difficult in order to stimulate the advanced cognitive processes needed to overcome intercultural differences. It's a case of 'no pain, no gain' – cognitively speaking.

So far I've argued that to enhance creativity, intercultural contact should be *immersive*, and involve *dual engagement* as well as groups that espouse significant *cultural differences*. These conditions provide the basis for understanding not only when but *how* such experiences can stimulate creative thought: these key conditions require us to adopt a different way of thinking in order to psychologically engage with cultural perspectives different from our own. Understanding the thought processes people adopt in these situations is the key to understanding how intercultural contact stimulates creative cognition. Most importantly, they provide a road map for how to best structure intercultural contact so as to harness the benefits of coalitional thinking in the social brain.

FRAME-SWITCHING

The first way individuals can deal cognitively with diversity is what I refer to as *frame-switching*: cross-cultural researchers have found that bicultural individuals deal with frequent intercultural contact by alternating between the two cultural frames. We know that bicultural people who have become adept at cultural frame-switching are able to shift easily between different cultural perspectives, depending on which context they find themselves in. For instance, one study of 2002[94] showed that Chinese-American biculturals who were shown images designed to bring the USA to mind – burgers, the Stars and Stripes, the Statue of Liberty and so forth – subsequently thought in a more Western style: that is, they focused on the individual. In contrast, bicultural participants shown images that brought China to mind, such as noodles, the Chinese flag and the Great Wall, subsequently thought in a more East Asian cultural style; that's to say, they focused on the collective.

Evidence suggests that this ability to frame-switch could be responsible for the typically observed boosts in biculturals' creative performance. The ability to rapidly and effortlessly switch between different perspectives is a key component of creative cognition. For instance, in another classic divergent-thinking task, people are asked to generate different uses for a plastic bottle. If they come up with such suggestions as 'to hold liquid' or 'to drink from' – in other words, their answers are restricted to one conceptual category – they are categorised as less original. On the other hand, being able to jump between different categories of meaning yields more diverse ideas, such as 'to use as a piggy bank' (storage), or 'to put flowers in' (ornament). So when in the course of intercultural contact people have to shift between cultural perspectives as just outlined, the exercise tones up this cognitive ability, which is, as noted, central to creative performance.

CONCEPTUAL INTEGRATION

While frame-switching may at first be ideally suited to negotiating intercultural communication, as time goes by it will prove more adaptive to adopt a more efficient way of thinking. Specifically, no matter how adept one becomes at frame-switching, one frame is easier to handle than two. Certainly, integrating cultural perspectives so as to form a new, shared identity provides meaning, clarity and predictability – all things the human mind craves. But to integrate takes real cognitive effort, and notwithstanding the commonalities, the individual has to reconcile the unavoidable conflicts and differences that exist between cultures (especially when cultural distance is maximal).

Recall that in Chapter 6 we saw that intercultural experiences require individuals to cognitively reconcile differences between cultural perspectives. I also described there my own research in which I asked the participants to conceptually integrate stereotypes that are not usually seen to go together, such as 'a woman' who is also 'an engineer'.

When conflicting information like this is conceptually integrated and inconsistencies resolved, a revised impression of the cultural outgroup is formed. This impression will necessarily be less reliant on stereotypes, and instead based on prospection, as discussed earlier. Importantly, this inconsistency-resolving process represents an overlapping – and key – cognitive element of creative thinking. This is because the processes required to reconcile inconsistencies between cultures are also central to generating new ideas, and in particular the ability to inhibit existing knowledge in favour of something new. Research on learning has shown that individuals tend to employ a model of conflict resolution that has been useful in the past, even though that model has been removed from its original context. If the resolution technique is repeated and positively reinforced, it will become the person's dominant response style when he or she negotiates new situations. Thus, over time, resolving the conflicts highlighted by intercultural experiences will engender a tendency to adopt the same strategies when he or she encounters contexts requiring the same abilities.

Now, as I've noted, intercultural experiences often require us to resolve conflicts to do with values, ideas, customs and attitudes – particularly when they involve engagement with an outgroup culture. This should trigger the process of inconsistency-resolution described above, which, if repeated and reinforced, can enhance creativity. Research on creativity supports this idea. For instance, participants who were asked questions that encouraged the combining of concepts (for instance, what kind of vehicle can travel on land and on water?) ended up building LEGO models that were rated as more original and innovative than those built by other participants who hadn't been asked such questions.[95]

The benefits of conceptual integration may be particularly pronounced in creativity tests tailored to capture an

over-reliance on existing knowledge. For instance, when asked
to generate new names for pasta (as we saw in Chapter 6) or
chemicals, individuals will often copy exemplars given in
the test instructions, resulting in what's called 'inadvertent
plagiarism'.[96] Intercultural experiences should practise precisely the ability to conceptually integrate that is characteristic
of creative thinking. The repeated reconciliation of conflicting
values, customs and ideas will render individuals better able to
banish existing knowledge when trying to generate new ideas.

ADAPTATION OVER TIME

Three characteristics of intercultural contact are required to
stimulate the coalitional thinking system: the experience must
be immersive, involve dual engagement and include categories
that are culturally distinct. When these conditions are met, distinct cognitive strategies can be employed, all of which can
come to benefit creative performance in different ways.
Individuals may frame-switch between cultures. They may
conceptually integrate cultural frames to resolve conflicts con-
cerning values, customs and attitudes. Finally, they may come
to construe more inclusive relations between the groups.

These characteristics are not mutually exclusive; rather, it's
that over time they progressively open the door to different
components of the coalitional thinking system. This developmental model of cognitive adaptation is consistent with recent
research on how experiences of diversity come to be in-
corporated into one's concept of self. People who have gained
intercultural experience usually talk about it as being self-
defining – the experience has become a part of *who they are*,
internalised. Research has shown that as we develop wider

social networks and, in particular, networks that involve diverse and differentiated features for us to identify with, we evolve a more complex social identity – an integrated self-concept – that includes all the disparate identities. In the context of intercultural contact this means conceptually integrating cultural perspectives, as I've discussed. Importantly, the different cognitive strategies and consequences may be triggered at different points in this adaptation process.

At first, the individual involved in intercultural contact is unlikely to attempt the challenging process of conceptual integration. They are more likely to start with switching between cultural perspectives as an initial stage of cognitive adaptation. Intercultural perceivers will be highly sensitive to the social ecology around them, and so as to smooth early coalitional negotiations they will develop frame-switching abilities to enable them to alternate between their own and the outgroup's perspective.

As time goes by, they will become increasingly aware of the conflicts to do with values, customs, ideologies and culture that exist between the ingroup and the outgroup. Skills of conceptual integration will be required of them in order to resolve these conflicts. In so doing, these individuals will become ever more adept at integrating cultural perspectives, at inhibiting existing knowledge and generating new ideas.

SUMMARY

In this chapter I've proposed a detailed model of how intercultural contact, over time, can stimulate coalitional thinking. Based on this developmental analysis, cumulative and qualitatively distinct benefits for creativity can be predicted, depending on the length of time people spend engaged in inter-cultural contact. The experience must be immersive and involve dual engagement as well as categories that are cultur-ally distinct. As people progress, engagement with one's own and the outgroup's cultural perspectives will prompt further ways of thinking creatively. Frame-switching will bring enhanced sensitivity to the different cultural cues that exist in one's social environment. This will enable an enhanced cap-acity to adapt to whatever is the cultural norm in the situation at hand. As people begin to conceptually integrate conflicting cultural values, norms and ideologies, they'll develop an enhanced capacity to inhibit learned expectations in favour of new and original ideas. Eventually a new and integrated sense of self will have been achieved, one that has taught the intercultural perceiver, along the way, a range of cognitive operations that will quite literally have broadened the mind.

CHAPTER 10

ON WEALTH, HEALTH AND HAPPINESS

In this book I've argued that one of the most significant events in human prehistory, the Great Leap Forward, can be explained by intercultural contact. The advances in human cognition, which spurred social, economic and technological advances, coincided with our ancestors' migration out of Africa. Many evolutionary psychologists have located at this point the explanation for our propensity for intercultural conflict. They suggest that our discontentment with diversity – manifest as prejudice, discrimination, anti-immigration sentiment, political unrest and even inter-ethnic war – is part of our evolutionary heritage; that it can be traced back to a time when our ancestors' survival depended on the strength of their group, or tribal collective; a time when other human tribes represented a significant threat to our survival.

Some evidence supports this view. Psychological science has shown that outgroups often fail to activate parts of the brain that are usually activated during social interaction. This suggests that outgroups are seen as somehow less than human by our brains' threat-detection system. Indeed, it takes longer to unlearn negative associations with outgroup members than with our ingroup counterparts – an adaptive trait that keeps us appropriately wary of those from groups different from our own.

The most recent studies have, however, revealed that these dehumanisation tendencies are not so hardwired and that they can be altered by positive intercultural experiences. It's suggested that the predominance of the threat-detection system is not absolute, and that the coalitional thinking system evolved to help our ancestors adapt to diversity. I have argued that, where outgroups are concerned, this shift from a focus on threat to a focus on coalition shows that humans evolved not always to seek fight or flight but also to cooperate, build bridges, foster allies and forge alliances. This was a critical step in the making of the modern mind because it accelerated the evolution of creative cognition – our ability to innovate, to envisage a future world full of possibility and potential.

So in many situations the most adaptive outcome for our ancestors may have been not to compete, but to co-operate with other groups. It is this ability to look beyond difference, to adapt to, not eschew, diversity, that may even have been the basis for the evolution of complex civilisation, the basis for cultural progress and technological advance. A sole system devoted to conflict could not have enabled the group to flourish and grow, and eventually become the society we know. We had to have a second cognitive system for adapting to diversity.

Of course, it's self-evident that humans are not *only* coalition builders. Default systems of thinking still compel outgroup aggression, as the wars and other conflicts of the twentieth and twenty-first centuries show all too clearly. But modern psychological science has identified ways of accessing the coalitional thinking system, as we've seen. Crucially, and predicating my argument on the unique set of cognitive abilities needed to build coalitions, I believe that harnessing this system can help us not only to establish harmonious intercultural relations but also to maximise the human capacity for cognitive growth. In this final chapter I speculate that properly structured intercultural contact, of the sort described in Chapter 9, can train the brain in just the same way as any muscle. In so doing, a capacity for enhanced performance may be encouraged and exploited in a range of personal, social and organisational domains.

In the previous chapter I argued that while prospection provided the necessary kick-start to coalitional thinking, it was the cognitive-adaptation processes following on from real intercultural contact that made the modern mind. This stems from the fact that increasingly immersive, engaging and challenging contact makes possible a process of cognitive adaptation that stimulates – and requires – a high degree of flexibility. This cognitive flexibility comprises at first the ability to switch between cultural frames. Later it becomes the ability to inhibit existing cultural perspectives and conceptually integrate different customs and values'. The critical end point of this adaptation process is an enhanced ability to put aside stereotypes and negative expectations about different groups, and instead to engage, with an open mind, in building positive relations. This ability to put aside existing knowledge, expectations and norms is also the key ingredient of creativity – and in many different spheres of life. This has come about because inhibitory control can, in broad terms, be thought of as impulse control – something that for many people is key to self-improvement, whether in the realms of academic study (resisting the impulse to party), health (resisting the impulse to eat cake) or relationships (biting your tongue when your partner annoys you!).

Below I speculate on some of the ways in which enhanced inhibitory or impulse control, triggered by the experience of extended intercultural contact, could promote wealth, health and happiness. I focus on four hypothesised areas in which benefit should accrue, all of them linked by their dependence on inhibitory or impulse control. If our repeatedly engaging in intercultural contact can train, refine and strengthen this form of cognitive control, then we should detect as a result, in all of these areas, significant improvement in performance.

FINANCIAL DECISION-MAKING

It's well established that people's poor ability to estimate risk in financial decisions is a result of an inability to inhibit or resist impulse. In particular, clinical and neuropsychological studies indicate that in financial decision-making the dorsolateral prefrontal cortex, a region linked to inhibitory ability, plays a significant role. Damage to this prefrontal region leads to difficulties in financial management: individuals with such an impairment make poor, risky choices and are often unable to inhibit current desires or impulses, or take longer-term views when making financial choices. Neuro-imaging studies also indicate that prefrontal inhibitory systems are involved in the processing of financial information in healthy individuals.

If intercultural contact stimulates the social brain and enhances inhibitory control, in financial affairs it should help individuals resist the first impulse that comes to mind and instead think more about the decision at hand. This capability lies at the heart of the biases in financial decision-making noted above. For even stronger evidence we can delve deeper into the psychology of these biases. For instance, a phenomenon referred to as 'temporal discounting' describes people's inability to inhibit immediate, but less beneficial, outcomes in the present in favour of larger benefits in the future – a tendency that has a direct detrimental impact on savings, investment and retirement planning. Temporal discounting can therefore influence how people perceive and appraise their current situation and the risks and benefits that their current behaviour holds for the future. Inhibiting the present and imagining a different future – or alternative possible futures – could enable individuals to envisage, and attain, a better pecuniary future.

PHYSICAL HEALTH

People are remarkably bad at preventative health. For instance, some stats show that after initiating exercise regimes only 50 per cent are still exercising after six months. Fewer than half of those who quit smoking are still abstaining after twelve months. After a year, only 25 per cent of those who start dieting plans are still dieting. People know the risks of poor diet, lack of exercise, unprotected sex, UV exposure, smoking and drinking, yet they seem unable to engage in the sort of preventative behaviour that is called for to mitigate these risks.

Much work has shown that inhibitory ability is a critical determinant of people's poor health behaviour. In particular, socio-cognitive models of self-regulation have inhibitory ability at their core. Here again people are typically unable to inhibit their immediate needs and impulses – they remain rooted in the moment rather than projecting themselves into the future and imagining the possible negative consequences of

their current behaviour, or the positive consequences of changing it. Adapting to diversity – and the enhanced inhibitory
control it brings – should help people avoid temporal discounting in terms of both financial and health planning. And given
that research has identified failures of impulse control as a
common mechanism underlying problems in both financial and
health decision-making, intercultural contact may help train
our brains to break out of these negative cycles, habits and
norms.

SUSTAINABLE CONSUMPTION

As well as helping us to achieve personal goals, diversity may
help communities work together on issues that affect us all. In
our world billions are without clean drinking water, millions
are malnourished, and debt, deforestation, pollution and global
warming present distinct dangers to the continuation of our
civilisation. Some predictions suggest that if the current rate of
consumption continues, global oil reserves will be seriously
depleted within forty years. With households contributing over
40 per cent of the world's carbon emissions, finding ways to
encourage sustainable consumption is a critical challenge for
our generation.

Why, then, do people fail to act on environmental issues?
Much like the biases described above in financial and health
planning, their inability to inhibit current needs can discourage
them from taking action on long-term challenges such as
climate change. Our improved inhibitory abilities arising from
diversity experiences should therefore also increase our
engagement with environmental issues. Better environmental
planning requires the ability not only to inhibit one's own

current needs and impulses, but also to inhibit one's own needs in favour of collective needs. In other words, it is about resisting self-interest and acting in the common good.

Observing typical behaviour during fuel shortages illustrates the point. When governments issue an appeal for restraint because of a sudden gap in supply, the individual has a choice. Either people maintain, as asked, their usual pattern of fuel consumption, filling up only when needed; or they rush out and fill up their petrol tank in anticipation of the shortage. If everyone does the former there will be enough fuel to go round; if everyone does the latter the sudden surge in demand will exacerbate the shortage, possibly causing pumps to run dry. Again, the challenge for the individual is to resist the urge to act self-interestedly and stock up with as much fuel as possible; this requires substantial inhibitory-control of precisely the sort involved in coalitional thinking. The same logic applies when we receive appeals to reduce our carbon footprint: we can simply ignore them and carry on living a convenient, carbon-filled life – but then everyone will ultimately suffer the collective cost of escalating emissions.

We find it hard to inhibit the strong concrete needs of now in favour of the more remote, abstract needs of future generations. Adapting to diversity in the here and now can bolster our self-control and help us resist the impulse to consume in a purely self-interested way.

EQUALITY AND EMPOWERMENT

In business one area that stimulates great debate is gender equality. In Britain, statistics show that around two-thirds of managers and senior officials are men, whereas four out of five people in administrative and secretarial roles are women. Likewise, the majority of people in skilled trades are men while the majority in service roles such as healthcare and childcare are women. Women constitute just 1 per cent of apprentices in the construction industry and men less than 1 per cent in the child-care sector.[97] One of the problems with such differentials is that they discourage individuals from entering fields of study or occupation purely because of their minority status: a state of affairs that's compounded by psychological barriers caused by social stereotyping. However, research has shown that when women take on characteristically male roles they come to display enhanced creative performance consistent with the principles outlined in this book. The argument can readily be extended to the creative benefits of gender diversity in the boardroom.

Diversity in business works because it stimulates the social brain, and with this comes all the benefits of creativity: flexi-bility, fresh perspectives and the propensity to see things differently from how they are.

SUMMARY

In this chapter I've speculated on how the benefits of inter-cultural contact could extend to a range of areas in everyday life. Central to this is cognitive inhibition, or impulse control. According to well-established learning principles, repeatedly engaging in cognitive inhibition will improve the individual's ability to resist impulsive behaviour generally. Extended immersive intercultural contact should train the social brain's inhibitory muscle, with diverse benefits resulting. For instance, saving for one's retirement involves inhibiting the current desire to spend and forgoing immediate gratification. A healthy lifestyle requires inhibiting the urge to eat high-fat foods. Engaging in environmentally positive behaviour requires inhibiting one's self-interest with a view to protecting resources for future generations. Achieving success in business requires inhibiting the impact of negative stereotypes on confidence and aspiration. Promoting behavioural change in all these areas is central to fostering a fitter, happier and more productive society.

If the propositions outlined in this book are correct, then this behaviour change will be linked to, and to a great extent dependent upon, harnessing the potential lying latent in our social brains.

EPILOGUE

In this book I've talked about the psychology of social cognition – how who we are, and what we think is defined by the diversity inherent in our social worlds. I've explained political and public discontent with diversity, why there's a widespread belief that multiculturalism has 'failed'; and why, at our most basic, we prefer simplicity, structure and clarity over complexity, difference and diversity. Our outgroup threat-detection system is an early-evolved mechanism for detecting who is 'us' and who is 'them'. But I've also highlighted another way in which our ancestors' minds were forged through intercultural contact – how cooperation, not conflict, shaped a second cognitive system. This second system has enabled us to build bridges with people from other groups, to resist the impulse to use stereotypes and other biases; to envisage a world where diversity integrates, strengthens and solidifies our connections with one other.

So, while we may have evolved to think about people categorically, we also possess the computational mechanics to bypass this system when it's necessary to suppress, update or revise our stereotypes – that is, to deal with exceptions to the rule. Such a system offers an adaptive advantage, a cognitive capability for building new alliances in a world otherwise overrun by outgroups and conflict. In so doing it furnishes us with the ability to think creatively, providing the building blocks for great feats of human civilisation and technological innovation.

The implications of this analysis extend beyond the individual, to the social and the political. My intention has not been to offer a particular political view, but there are profound implications in my psychological analysis that may, and perhaps should, provide the starting point for a new and extended debate on the value of diversity and multiculturalism for modern society. Is increasing social diversity a good thing? Should politicians, policy makers and the public welcome our increasingly pluralist society?

These are questions that have dominated scholarly, political and public discourse in the early years of the twenty-first century. The argument I offer here contributes to the debate by linking notions of how and when tolerance can be achieved with a range of practical insights for individuals' personal and professional lives. The cutting-edge research I have discussed shows how the experience of social and cultural diversity can yield benefits for individuals and for societies, and on very real psychological, social and economic dimensions. Understanding the ways in which those benefits are to be realised is critical to explicating the importance of multiculturalism for modern societies.

Uncovering the link between diversity and what I've called coalitional thinking also feeds into specific debates on education policy. Opponents of multiculturalism say that getting children to think about diversity issues distracts them from the true aim of education – to foster academic excellence. The idea of the social brain challenges these views, indicating that diversity is absolutely key to academic attainment. This suggests it should feature in schools as a core component of the curriculum.

As well as providing scientific justification for multicultural policies, the scientific studies that continue to elucidate the link between diversity and coalitional thinking will offer new ways to develop at psychologically informed interventions for promoting tolerance. According to the evidence and the ideas discussed in this book, intercultural contact can not only help promote tolerance, it can also foster innovation and original thinking. Further exploring these and other benefits of intercultural communication will open up new avenues for future research and practical application.

The research discussed here has shown that while multiculturalism can enrich modern society, human nature compels widespread rejection of this inherently complex concept. People prefer environments low in social complexity. I've suggested, however, that there is hitherto untapped promise and potential in embracing social and cultural diversity, in both our personal and our professional lives. I argue that to promote more positive intercultural relations we must devise a public policy that will switch on coalitional thinking in the social brain. For instance, strategies that embrace diversity should help nurture creativity and cognitive flexibility. The implication is that intercultural contact can encourage people to embrace innovative ideas.

Yes, the status quo is comforting, but it is unlikely to yield the new perspectives needed to stimulate progress and change. And in our challenging economic times embracing diversity may be essential in order to trigger new approaches to economic growth. In short, the phenomena described in this book suggest that valuing diversity is not merely moral, right or humanitarian: at a time when the world has just experienced one of the worst financial crises in living memory, it is economically and politically expedient.

Behavioural science has not traditionally contributed to these sorts of debate, but here I have shown that it offers some empirically established principles that are highly relevant to the social and political issues of today. According to these principles, prospection – the ability to envisage a world different from the one we know – can be harnessed. This, and associated abilities that the experience of diversity will elicit over time, may well result in general improvements to creative cognition.

Furthermore, because these abilities are central to a range of everyday concerns involving judgement and decision-making, adapting to diversity has wide-reaching implications. For instance, research has revealed that the experience of diversity can contribute to cognitive development. Studies of decision-making have found that culturally heterogeneous groups tend to reject simple and obvious solutions to problems in favour of solutions that incorporate multiple perspectives: the result is that better decisions are made. Studies in the field of cross-cultural psychology show how immigrants for whom intercultural contact is a familiar and frequent occurrence think more abstractly, are able to draw on these multiple perspectives and are better at comparing and contrasting ideas. And of course, understanding the origins, function and scope of the psychological systems I've discussed may be particularly important in tackling human conflict.

However, the true message of this book resonates much deeper. It is that diversity in our social ecologies can help us to nurture a more creative, resilient and adaptive culture. Future policy designed to harness coalitional thinking in us all may well help promote positive relations between communities. But it may also have the potential to improve our everyday decision-making in many different aspects of our lives – from the professional to the physical and to the psychological. Diversity develops creative minds in compelling us to think beyond norms and conventions, to 'think outside the box'.

Just as I've argued that diversity has been pivotal to our intellectual evolution, so it may ultimately become a defining feature of our societies' future prosperity, progress and growth. We must strive to understand how our brains navigate diverse social ecologies, tap into those latent systems and use the knowledge gained to inform, focus and frame policy and practice. Perhaps only by understanding and harnessing these systems can we unlock the door to the next great leap in human evolution.

NOTES

INTRODUCTION

1. BBC News (2010). *Merkel says German multicultural society has failed.* Retrieved from http://www.bbc.co.uk/news/world-europe-11559451

2. BBC News (2011). *State multiculturalism has failed, says David Cameron.* Retrieved from http://www.bbc.co.uk/news/uk-politics-12371994

3. BBC News (2010). *Merkel says German multicultural society has failed.* Retrieved from http://www.bbc.co.uk/news/world-europe-11559451

4. European Monitoring Centre on Racism and Xenophobia (2005). *Majorities' attitudes towards migrants and minorities: Key findings from the Eurobarometer and the European Social Survey.* Retrieved from: http://fra.europa.eu/fra/material/pub/eurobarometer/EB2005/EB2005-summary.pdf

5. Sky News (2013). *Illegal immigration in US now hard to ignore.* Retrieved from http://news.sky.com/story/1154076/illegal-immigration-in-US-now-hard-to-ignore

6. Kahneman, D. (2011). *Thinking Fast and Slow.* Penguin: London.

CHAPTER 1

7. United Nations/Organisation for Economic Co-operation and Development (2013). *World migration in figures*. Retrieved from http://www.oecd.org/els/mig/World-Migration-in-Figures.pdf

8. US Census Bureau (2014). *New census bureau statistics show how young adults today compare with previous generations in neighborhoods nationwide*. Retrieved from http://www.census.gov/newsroom/press-releases/2014/cb14-219.html

9. Office for National Statistics (2013). *Immigration patterns of non-UK-born populations in England and Wales in 2011*. Retrieved from http://www.ons.gov.uk/ons/dcp171776_346219.pdf

10. BBC News (2013). *Why have the white British left London?* Retrieved from http://www.bbc.co.uk/news/uk-21511904

11. Home Office (2012). *Hate crimes, England and Wales 2011–2012*. Retrieved from https://www.gov.uk/government/statistics/hate-crimes-england-and-wales-2011-to-2012

12. BBC News (2001). *Bradford's race divisions condemned*. Retrieved from http://news.bbc.co.uk/1/hi/uk/1435062.stm

13. US Census Bureau (2008). *An older and more diverse nation by mid-century*. Retrieved from http://www.census.gov/PressRelease/www/releases/ archives/population/012496.html

14. Plaut, V. C. (2010). Diversity science: Why and how difference makes a difference, *Psychological Inquiry*, 77, 85–90.

15. Equalities Review (2007). *Fairness and freedom: The final report of the Equalities Review*. Retrieved from http://archive.cabinetoffice.gov.uk/equalitiesreview/

16. Pew Research Centre for Global Attitudes and Trends (2006). *Muslims in Europe: Economic worries top concerns about religious and cultural identity*. Retrieved from http://www.pewglobal.org/2006/07/06/muslims-in-europe-economic-worries-top-concerns-about-religious-and-cultural-identity/

17. Huntington, S. P. (1993). The Clash of Civilizations? *Foreign Affairs*, *72*, 22.

18. Freud, S. (1929/2002). *Civilization and Its Discontents*. London, Penguin.

19. Adorno, T. W., Frenkel-Brunswik, E., Levinson, D. J., & Sanford, R. N. (1950). *The Authoritarian Personality*. New York, Harper and Row (p. 228).

20. Hovland, C. I., & Sears, R. R. (1940). Minor studies in aggression: VI. Correlation of lynchings with economic indices. *Journal of Psychology*, *9*, 301–10.

21. Blanchard, F. A., Adelman, L., & Cook, S. W. (1975). Effect of group success and failure upon interpersonal attraction in cooperating interracial groups. *Journal of Personality and Social Psychology*, *31*, 1020–30.

22. Greenberg, J., Pyszczynski, T., Solomon, S., Rosenblatt, A., Veeder, M., Kirkland, S., et al. (1990). Evidence for terror management II: The effects of mortality salience on reactions to those who threaten or bolster the cultural worldview. *Journal of Personality and Social Psychology*, *58*, 308–18.

23. Rios Morrison, K., Plaut, V. C., & Ybarra, O. (2010). Predicting whether multiculturalism positively or negatively influences White Americans' intergroup attitudes: The role of ethnic identification. *Personality and Social Psychology Bulletin*, *36*, 1648–61.

CHAPTER 2

24. Kelley, H. H., & Michela, J. L. (1980). Attribution theory and research. *Annual Review of Psychology*, *31*, 457–501.

25. Jones, E. E., & Harris, V. A. (1967). The attribution of attitudes. *Journal of Experimental Social Psychology*, *3*, 1–24.

26. Plous, S. (1989). Thinking the unthinkable: The effects of

anchoring on likelihood estimates of nuclear war. *Journal of Applied Social Psychology*, *19*, 67–91.

27. Dutton, D. G., & Aron, A. P. (1974). Some evidence for heightened sexual attraction under conditions of high anxiety. *Journal of Personality and Social Psychology*, *28*, 510–17.

28. Milgram, S. (1963). Behavioral study of obedience. *Journal of Abnormal and Social Psychology*, *67*, 371–8.

CHAPTER 3

29. Tajfel, H., Billig, M., Bundy, R., & Flament, C. (1971). Social categorization and intergroup behaviour. *European Journal of Social Psychology*, *1*, 149–78.

30. Cuddy, A., Rock, M., & Norton, M. (2007). Aid in the aftermath of Hurricane Katrina: Inferences of secondary emotions and intergroup helping. *Group Processes & Intergroup Relations*, *10*, 107–18.

31. Costello, K., & Hodson, G. (2010). Exploring the role of dehumanization: The role of animal–human similarity in promoting immigrant humanization. *Group Processes & Intergroup Relations*, *13*, 3–22.

32. Rubin, M., Paolini, S., & Crisp, R. J. (2011). The relationship between the need for closure and deviant bias: An investigation of generality and process. *International Journal of Psychology*, *46*, 206–13.

33. Staats, C. K., & Staats, A. W. (1958). Attitudes established by classical conditioning. *Journal of Abnormal and Social Psychology*, *57*, 37–40.

34. Phelps, E. A., O'Connor, K. J., Cunningham, W. A., Funayma, E. S., Gatenby, J. C., Gore, J. C., & Banaji, M. R. (2000). Performance on indirect measures of race evaluation predicts amygdala activity. *Journal of Cognitive Neuroscience*, *12*, 1–10.

35. Navarrete, C. D., Olsson, A., Ho., A. K., Mendes, W. B.,

Thomsen, L., & Sidanius, J. (2012). Fear extinction to an out-group face: The role of target gender. *Psychological Science, 20,* 155–8.

36. Faulkner, J., Schaller, M., Park, J. H., & Duncan, L. A. (2004). Evolved disease-avoidance mechanisms and contemporary xenophobic attitudes. *Group Processes & Intergroup Relations,* 7, 333–53.

37. Hodson, G., & Costello, K. (2007). Interpersonal disgust, ideological orientations, and dehumanization as predictors of intergroup attitudes. *Psychological Science,* 18, 691–8.

38. Olsson, A., Ebert, J. P, Banaji, M. R., & Phelps, E. A. (2005). The role of social group in the persistence of learned fear. *Science,* 309, 785–7.

CHAPTER 4

39. Allport, G. W. (1954). *The Nature of Prejudice.* Reading, MA: Addison-Wesley.

40. Gaertner, S. L., Mann, J. A., Murrell, A. J., & Dovidio, J. F. (1989). Reducing intergroup bias: The benefits of recategorization. *Journal of Personality and Social Psychology,* 57, 239–49.

41. Van Leeuwen, E., van Knippenberg, D., & Ellemers, N. (2003). Continuing and changing group identities: The effects of merging on social identification and ingroup bias. *Personality and Social Psychology Bulletin,* 26, 679–90.

42. Crisp, R. J., Stone, C. H., & Hall, N. R. (2006). Recategorization and subgroup identification: Predicting and preventing threats from common ingroups. *Personality and Social Psychology Bulletin,* 32, 230–43.

43. Hutter, R. R. C., & Crisp, R. J. (2005). The composition of category conjunctions. *Personality and Social Psychology Bulletin,* 31, 647–57.

44. Bigler, R. S., & Liben, L. S. (1993). A cognitive developmental approach to racial stereotyping and reconstructive memory in Euro-American children. *Child Development*, *64*, 1507–18.

CHAPTER 5

45. Beck, S. R., Apperly, I. A., Chappell, J., Guthrie, C., & Cutting, N. (2011). Making tools isn't child's play. *Cognition*, *119*, 301–6.
46. Herrmann, E., Call, J., Hernansez-Lloreda, M. V., Hare, B., & Tomasello, M. (2007). Humans have evolved specialised skills of social cognition: The cultural intelligence hypothesis. *Science*, *317*, 1360–6.
47. Dunbar, R. I. M. (1998). The Social Brain Hypothesis. *Evolutionary Anthropology*, *6*, 178–90.
48. Jolly, A. (2007). The social origins of mind. *Science*, 317, 1326–7.
49. Stringer, C. (2003). Human evolution: Out of Ethiopia. *Nature*, 423, 692–3, 695.
50. Diamond, J. (1997/2005). *Guns, Germs and Steel: A Short History of Everybody for the Last 13,000 Years*. London: Vintage.
51. Pinker, S. (2011). *The Better Angels of Our Nature: Why Violence Has Declined*. New York: Viking.

CHAPTER 6

52. Gutierrez, J., & Sameroff, A. (1990). Determinants of complexity in Mexican-American and Anglo-American mothers' conceptions of child development. *Child Development*, *61*, 384–94.
53. Benet-Martínez, V., Lee, F., & Leu, J. (2006). Biculturalism and

cognitive complexity: Expertise in cultural representations. *Journal of Cross-Cultural Psychology, 37,* 386–407.

54. Carringer, D. C. (1974). Creative thinking abilities of Mexican youth: The relationship of bilingualism. *Journal of Cross-Cultural Psychology, 5,* 492–504.

55. Kharkhurin, A. V. (2005). On the possible relationships between bilingualism, biculturalism and creativity: A cognitive perspective. *Dissertation Abstracts International: Section B: The Sciences and Engineering, 66,* 1766.

56. Maddux, W. W., & Galinsky, A. D. (2009). Cultural borders and mental barriers: The relationship between living abroad and creativity. *Journal of Personality and Social Psychology, 96,* 1047–61.

57. Leung, K. Y., & Chiu, C. Y. (2010). Multicultural experience, idea receptiveness and creativity. *Journal of Cross-Cultural Psychology, 41,* 723.

58. Leung, A. K.-Y., & Chiu, C.-Y. (2008). Interactive effects of multicultural experiences and openness to experience on creative potential. *Creativity Research Journal, 20,* 376–82.

59. Simonton, D. K. (1997). Foreign influence and national achievement: The impact of open milieus on Japanese civilization. *Journal of Personality and Social Psychology, 72,* 86–94.

60. Simonton, D. K. (1975). Sociocultural context of individual creativity: A transhistorical time-series analysis. *Journal of Personality and Social Psychology, 32,* 1119–33.

61. Simonton, D. K. (1976). Philosophical eminence, beliefs and zeitgeist: An individual-generational analysis. *Journal of Personality and Social Psychology, 34,* 630–40.

62. Hambrick, D., Cho, T., & Chen, M. (1996). The influence of top management team heterogeneity on firms' competitive moves. *Administrative Science Quarterly, 41,* 659–84.

63. Hamilton, B., Nickerson, J., & Owan, H. (2003). Team incentives and worker heterogeneity: An empirical analysis of the

impact of teams on productivity and participation. *Journal of Political Economy*, 111, 465–97.

64. Nemeth, C. J., & Wachtler, J. (1983). Creative problem solving as a result of majority vs minority influence. *European Journal of Social Psychology*, *13*, 45–55.

65. Nemeth, C. J. (1977). Interactions between jurors as a function of majority vs. unanimity decision rules. *Journal of Applied Social Psychology*, 7, 38–56.

66. Bigler, R. S., & Liben, L. S. (1992). Cognitive mechanisms in children's gender stereotyping: Theoretical and educational implications of a cognitive-based mechanism. *Child Development*, *63*, 1351–63.

67. Goclowska, M. A., Crisp, R. J., & Labuschagne, K. (2013). Can counter-stereotypes boost flexible thinking? *Group Processes & Intergroup Relations*, *16*, 217–31.

CHAPTER 7

68. Hovland, C. I., & Sears, R. R. (1940). Minor studies in aggression: VI. Correlation of lynchings with economic indices. *Journal of Psychology*, *9*, 301–10.

69. Levine, R. A., & Campbell, D. T. (1972). *Ethnocentrism: Theories of Conflict, Ethnic Attitudes and Group Behavior*. New York: Wiley.

70. Berry, J. W., & Annis, R. C. (1974). Acculturation stress: The role of ecology, culture and differentiation. *Journal of Cross-cultural Psychology*, *5*, 382–406.

71. Tsui, A. S., Egan, T. D., & O'Reilly, C. A., III. (1992). Being different: Relational demography and organisational attachment. *Administrative Science Quarterly*, *37*, 549–79.

72. Homan, A. C., van Knippenberg, D., van Kleef, G. A., & De Dreu, C. K. W. (2007). Bridging faultlines by valuing diversity: Diversity beliefs, information elaboration, and performance in

diverse work groups. *Journal of Applied Psychology*, *92*, 1189–99.

73. Kosslyn, S. M., Ganis, G., & Thompson, W. L. (2001). Neural foundations of imagery. *Nature Reviews Neuroscience*, *2*, 635–42.

74. Galinsky, A. D., & Moskowitz, G. B. (2000). Counterfactuals as behavioral primes: Priming the simulation heuristic and the consideration of alternatives. *Journal of Experimental Social Psychology*, *36*, 357–83.

75. Ratcliff, C. D., Czuchry, M., Scarberry, N. C., Thomas, J. C., Dansereau, D. F., & Lord, C. G. (1999). Effects of directed thinking on intentions to engage in beneficial activities: Actions versus reasons. *Journal of Applied Social Psychology*, *29*, 994–1009.

76. Sherman, S. J., & Anderson, C. A. (1987). Decreasing premature termination from psychotherapy. *Journal of Social and Clinical Psychology*, *5*, 298–312.

77. Driskell, J. E., Copper, C., & Moran, A. (1994). Does mental practice enhance performance? *Journal of Applied Psychology*, *79*, 481–91.

78. Holmes, E. A., & Mathews, A. (2010). Mental imagery in emotion and emotional disorders. *Clinical Psychology Review*, *30*, 349–62.

CHAPTER 8

79. Crisp, R. J., & Turner, R. N. (2009). Can imagined interactions produce positive perceptions? Reducing prejudice through simulated social contact. *American Psychologist*, *64*, 231–40.

80. Turner, R. N., Crisp, R. J., & Lambert, E. (2007). Imagining intergroup contact can improve intergroup attitudes. *Group Processes & Intergroup Relations*, *10*, 427–41.

81. Turner, R. N., & Crisp, R. J. (2010). Imagining intergroup

contact reduces implicit prejudice. *British Journal of Social Psychology*, *49*, 129–42.

82. Husnu, S., & Crisp, R. J. (2010). Elaboration enhances the imagined contact effect. *Journal of Experimental Social Psychology*, *46*, 943–950.

83. Husnu, S., & Crisp, R. J. (2010). Elaboration enhances the imagined contact effect. *Journal of Experimental Social Psychology*, *46*, 943–50.

84. Birtel, M. D., & Crisp, R. J. (2012). Imagining intergroup contact is more cognitively difficult for people higher in intergroup anxiety but this does not detract from its effectiveness. *Group Processes & Intergroup Relations*, *15*, 744–61.

85. Cameron, L., Rutland, A., Turner, R., Holman-Nicolas, R., & Powell, C. (2011). Changing attitudes with a little imagination: Imagined contact effects on young children's intergroup bias. *Anales de Psicología*, *27*, 708–17.

86. Vezzali, L., Capozza, D., Giovannini, D., & Stathi, S. (2012). Improving implicit and explicit intergroup attitudes using imagined contact: An experimental intervention with elementary school children. *Group Processes and Intergroup Relations*, *15*, 203–12.

87. Vezzali, L., Capozza, D., Stathi, S., & Giovannini, D. (2012). Increasing outgroup trust, reducing infrahumanization, and enhancing future contact intentions via imagined intergroup contact. *Journal of Experimental Social Psychology*, *48*, 437–40.

88. Husnu, S., & Crisp, R. J. (2011). Enhancing the imagined contact effect. *Journal of Social Psychology*, *151*, 113–16.

89. Crisp, R. J., & Husnu, S. (2011). Attributional processes underlying imagined contact effects. *Group Processes and Intergroup Relations*, *14*, 275–87.

90. Galinsky, A. D., & Moskowitz, G. B. (2000). Perspective-taking: Decreasing stereotype expression, stereotype accessibility, and

in-group favoritism. *Journal of Personality and Social Psychology, 78*, 708–24.

CHAPTER 9

91. Crisp, R. J., & Turner, R. N. (2011). Cognitive adaptation to the experience of social and cultural diversity. *Psychological Bulletin, 137*, 242–66.
92. Crisp, R. J., & Meleady, R. (2012). Adapting to a multicultural future. *Science, 336*, 853–5.
93. Goclowska, M. A., & Crisp, R. J. (2014). How dual identity processes foster creativity. *Review of General Psychology, 18*, 216–36.
94. Haritatos, J., & Benet-Martínez, V. (2002). Bicultural identities: The interface of cultural, personality, and socio-cognitive processes. *Journal of Research in Personality, 6*, 598–606.
95. Wan, W. W. N., & Chiu, C.-Y. (2002). Effects of novel conceptual combination on creativity. *Journal of Creative Behavior, 36*, 227–40.
96. Dijksterhuis, A., & Meurs, T. (2006). Where creativity resides: The generative power of unconscious thought. *Consciousness and Cognition, 15*, 135–46.

CHAPTER 10

97. Francis, B., Dalgety, J., & Archer, L. (2005). *Gender equality in work experience placements for young people* (Equal Opportunities Commission working paper). Retrieved from http://www.educationandemployers.org/wp-content/uploads/ 2014/06/gender-equality-in-work-experience-placements-lmu.pdf

INDEX

THE
IMPR⟳VEMENT
ZONE

Looking for life inspiration?

The Improvement Zone has it all, from **expert advice** on how to advance your **career** and boost your **business**, to improving your **relationships**, revitalising your **health** and developing your **mind**.

Whatever your goals, head to our website now.

www.improvementzone.co.uk

INSPIRATION ON THE MOVE

INSPIRATION DIRECT TO YOUR INBOX